MW00669234

# DISCOURSE

*Discourse* provides an inclusive platform for reasoned discussion and prescriptive analysis of issues of both international and domestic concern, while also including poetry, fiction, art and photography to illuminate the human condition. Its emphasis is on exploring a diversity of thought and perspectives from students, scholars, and practitioners. The purpose of *Discourse* is to provide an open forum for discussion of contemporary dilemmas, not as a vehicle with any specific political or intellectual agenda. The perspectives represented are solely those of the authors.

A STUDENT PUBLICATION
OF TUFTS UNIVERSITY
WWW.TUFTSGLOBALLEADERSHIP.ORG

# THE TUFTS INTERDISCIPLI

# DEDICATED TO THE POWER OF R EXCHANGE OF ID

A STUDENT PUBLICATION
OF TUFTS UNIVERSITY

NARY JOURNAL

ASON AND THE

EAS

# EDITOR'S INTRODU

In the last issue of *Discourse*, we argued our belief that if modern humanity's fragile existence has any hope for survival in the face of current global crises, we must first seriously dedicate ourselves to a more engaged, civil, and reasoned public dialogue.

This truth is even more critical today.

While the spectrum of pundits declare with absolute certainty that the U.S. economy is destined for either amelioration or Armageddon, the one-time masters of the universe declare with absolute ambiguity that they have no idea what the future holds. What is certain is that the world is changing and the decisions that are made today will have long-lasting effects.

# S CTION

The multitude of crises we faced last year have not disappeared with the collapse of the global financial system, they have worsened and grown more urgent. This depression is not cause to take our attention away from the other problems we face but rather reason to finally address them sincerely.

In times of crisis it is easy to look inward and forget the crises that may not seem to be immediately at our doorstep. In times of anxiety it is easy to forego discussion and defer to power, but it would be our folly either to pretend the conditions of others do not affect our own or to blindly follow our new government without reflection of past mistakes and reasoned examination of potential future policy.

In this spirit I am confident that you will find this issue diverse and intellectually challenging. Much of the content of this issue examines the relationship between state and society, the latter's loss of trust and faith in the former, and the human impact of these issues. Austin Siadak's cover feature offers a thorough and gripping account of the global food crisis, followed by Ashraf Ghani's on concerns about how the security development complex operates. Hannah Flamm's essay on the challenges of development and having an open discussion about mining in El Salvador both builds on Dr. Ghani's and leads into Saskia Sassen's discussion about the complexity of powerlessness. Jessica Herrmann's piece is a magnificent primer on the U.S. mortgage crisis, complementing one of Dr. Sassen's examples and offering an analysis of policy. Nichole Sobecki's photo essay on Pakistan offers a visual window into the current challenge of Pakistan. Samuel James and Jessica Anderson's pieces on the aftermath of conflict in Northern Uganda, provide a diverse look at how communities begin to rebuild and reclaim their histories. Moving from transitional justice in Uganda, Nathaniel Teichman's piece looks at the juvenile justice system in the US. The issues concludes with two pieces of slam poetry on US urban issues by Jesse Welch.

I am confident you will be challenged and engaged by the contents of this issue. Its quality is owed to our talented contributors and to Heather Barry and Sherman Teichman at the Institute for Global Leadership, to the design of de.MO and Giorgio Baravalle and Megan Hall, and to the sponsorship of the Tufts Community Union Senate, the Merrin Family Fund, and the Tufts Undergraduate Research Fund.

Thank you for reading,

Padden Guy Murphy
*Editor in Chief*

/ END

# DISCOURSE

# THE FORGOTTEN CRISIS

HOW HIGH FOOD PRICES
HAVE IMPOVERISHED
MILLIONS AND
THREATENED GOVERNMENTS

AUSTIN BLAIR SIADAK

DISCOURSE

THE FORGOTTEN CRISIS
HOW HIGH FOOD PRICES HAVE
IMPOVERISHED MILLIONS AND
THREATENED GOVERNMENTS

AUSTIN BLAIR SIADAK

11

2 OF 30

Austin Siadak is currently a junior at Tufts University majoring in International Relations with a focus on Global Conflict, Cooperation and Justice. He has been involved in many activities through the Institute for Global Leadership at Tufts, including the Institute's Synaptic Scholars Program and the 2007-2008 EPIIC Colloquium on Global Poverty and Inequality. In May 2008, Austin investigated the effects of the global food crisis on the poor as a final EPIIC research project.

Author's Note

This essay was originally submitted in May of last year as a final research project for the 2007-2008 EPIIC Colloquium on Global Poverty and Inequality and was updated in late August, slated for publication in *Discourse*. Just weeks later, however, Lehman Brothers went bankrupt, marking the beginning of what has subsequently turned into a global financial crisis on a scale not seen for decades, perhaps ever. This crisis has wrought massive change across a multitude of regions, sectors and disciplines in past months, turning previously accepted practices into laughable follies and forcing all of us to rethink what we know about our modern world and how it works. It should thus come as no surprise that some of the information and situations explained in the following pages have changed since September – I must admit that when I was approached to update the piece for this semester I thought much of what I had written would be inapplicable or outdated under current circumstances. Despite these fears, I found that the current financial crisis has added more problems and difficulties to the food crisis than it has removed. Yes, some of the data has changed and the international environment is undoubtedly different now, but I have opted to leave the essay largely untouched to provide a clear understanding of one of the largest untold stories of the past few years that fails to disappear despite shifting international attention. Aware of the need for up-to-date information, I have added a short addendum describing the current state of the global food crisis.

Introduction

On April 21, 2008, Jacques Edouard Alexis was ousted from his position as Haitian Prime Minister following numerous violent clashes between United Nations troops and protestors calling for his removal.[1] To anyone familiar with Haitian history and politics, such an event might not seem extraordinary, given the frequent government overthrows, deadly insecurity, and near constant fighting that have plagued the country for the past few decades. What is extraordinary, however, was the cause of the deadly protests: food. Rising food prices had caused the costs of basic staples to run so high – pasta and rice prices had doubled in the past few months – that many poor, urban Haitians were reduced to buying and consuming "pica" – cookies made from salt, vegetable shortening, and dirt.[2] No wonder Haitians had rioted; they could afford nothing more than dirt, and some could not even afford that.

Unfortunately, this episode in Haiti is merely one of the many examples of how skyrocketing food prices have swept the globe and created havoc in the past year. For decades, the world benefited from cheap food, permitting hundreds of millions to move out of poverty and the global middle class to boom.[3] Now, however, that has all changed. From Cameroon to China, Pakistan to the Philippines, the fast rising costs of basic foodstuffs have made riots commonplace and left governments caught off guard in their attempts to stabilize prices, feed their people, and avoid both humanitarian and political catastrophes. Worse, hundreds of millions of impoverished peoples face the threat of malnutrition or starvation

DISCOURSE

THE FORGOTTEN CRISIS
HOW HIGH FOOD PRICES HAVE
IMPOVERISHED MILLIONS AND
THREATENED GOVERNMENTS

AUSTIN BLAIR SIADAK

13

4 OF 30

because they simply cannot afford to buy enough food, and it is very likely that global poverty reduction efforts may halt or even be reversed. Moreover, this is not just a problem confined to poor and developing states, as even the United States and European countries have seen large increases in the costs of their food, putting pressure on their populations and economies as well. The simple fact is that the world currently faces a truly *global* food crisis. Perhaps the most frightening aspect is that many experts predict this current wave of high prices to last for years to come, with the potential to leave lasting devastation in its wake.

Though the era of cheap food is over, many pressing questions remain. What caused the sudden jumps in prices? Who will be the most affected? How long will these new prices last? Who, if anyone, is benefiting from the current food crisis? And perhaps most importantly, what can be done right now to prevent humanitarian emergencies and to stabilize prices at an affordable rate for the majority of the world's consumers? This article will attempt to shed light on these questions, in addition to others, by providing an overview of the current global food crisis, what causes led to its existence, what repercussions are likely both in the short and long term, and some of the ways in which the peoples and governments of the world can best address this burgeoning disaster.

Cheap No More[4]

Before delving into the causes and long term implications of the global food crisis, it is important to understand the complex series of events that comprise the current predicament, including how much food prices have changed, what some of the most immediate effects have been, who is being affected the most, and who is profiting.

First, some history is in order. Until the past few years, food prices around the world had been extremely cheap for decades. Owing in large part to the Green Revolution that took place in the years after World War II, in which the use of improved technologies such as pesticides, advanced irrigation projects and synthetic fertilizers was widely increased in developing countries, global food output

increased dramatically. For example, the global cereal output alone doubled between 1961 and 1985.[5] Though oil crises and high inflation in the 1970s briefly caused food prices to shoot up, ever increasing production, technological innovation, increases in global crop acreage, market liberalization, and dropping oil prices sent food prices tumbling again in the last two decades of the century. For example, wheat prices topped $25 a bushel in the mid-1970s but had dropped to only $3 a bushel in 2000, adjusted for inflation.[6] This is not to say that food shortages, famine, and starvation were nonexistent during this period, but the overwhelming result was a worldwide boon for consumers who had access to both an increased amount and variety of foods. This included tens of millions of poor families who could attain better nutrition at a lower cost, greatly helping to reduce global poverty. However, at the same time, low prices meant that many farmers around the globe faced tougher times and often received less for their crops than did their parents in previous generations, increasing rural poverty in some areas.[7] Still, as the world rode the wave of cheap food into the new millennium, few predicted that large price changes would occur any time soon, much less to the degree that they did.[8]

Increases in the price of food over the past few years have not just been large, they have been astronomical. From 2005 to 2008, world food prices as a whole rose by 80 percent.[9] While this figure alone is alarming, hidden within it are much more recent and much larger price changes in some of the world's most important food crops. Foods made from cereal crops such as rice, wheat, or maize (corn) are consumed by nearly everyone on the planet, and for the world's poorest people these crops signify the large majority of their diet.[10] Thus, one can imagine how problematic it was when, in 2007 alone, wheat prices rose by 77 percent and rice prices rose by 16 percent. Even more worrisome were the massive jumps in the first few months of 2008, with rice prices in April rising 141 percent above their highest 2007 levels.[11] It is not just the price of cereals that has shot up either. Dairy prices have risen by nearly a third since the beginning of 2007, and oils and fats (used extensively for cooking around the world) are up 98 percent from March of 2007.[12] Though prices have dipped a bit since April and May of 2008, such increases are still unprecedented, and as one grain trader

For those living on $2 a day, it means cutting out meat from their diets and removing children from school. For those on $1 a day, it means removing meat and vegetables and eating only cereals. And for those living on 50 cents a day, in Sheeran's words, "it means total disaster."

tellingly puts it, "Anyone who tells you they've seen something like this is a liar."[13]

The most obvious effect of these price increases, and likely the worst, has been the drastic increase in the percentage of income that must be spent on food. While all consumers have had to pay more for food in the past year, the effects of increased spending are extremely unequal depending on one's income and location. A few more dollars for certain products may not make much of a difference to consumers in developed states, but it is often the difference between life and death for poorer populations who already pay heavily (comparatively) for more meager rations. Americans, for example, on average only spend about ten percent of household income on food. While increasing food prices may force these consumers to buy cheaper products or reduce spending in other sectors, they generally have the fortunate ability simply to shift where they spend their disposable income and continue their daily routines with little change.[14] Of course, this is not true for all, and many Americans are now finding it harder to make paychecks stretch far enough to cover high living costs and rising inflation, but very few face risks of starvation or severe malnutrition.

The same cannot be said for the world's poor. Because they already use a significant portion of their income to pay for food and have little disposable income, high food prices cause the poor to consume less nutritious foods and to reduce their overall food intake, leading to serious dietary and health problems. The International Food Policy Research Institute (IFPRI), a leading consulting and policy advising organization, notes that in general, "At the household level, the poor spend about 50 to 60 percent of their overall budget on food. For a five-person household living on US$1 per person per day, a 50 percent increase in food prices removes up to US$1.50 from their US$5 budget, and growing energy costs also add to their adjustment burden."[15] It is no wonder then that the price increases noted above, which far exceed rates of 50 percent, pose threats not just to diets and nutrition but to overall purchasing power as well, reducing the ability of the poor to afford sanitation, education, and healthcare. Moreover, because the poor generally buy primary products rather than processed foods (buying a kilo of maize rather than a box of Corn Flakes, for example) they are much more acutely affected by even small price increases.[16] Specifically, says Josette Sheeran, who runs the United Nations' World Food Programme (WFP), the impact

DISCOURSE

THE FORGOTTEN CRISIS
HOW HIGH FOOD PRICES HAVE
IMPOVERISHED MILLIONS AND
THREATENED GOVERNMENTS

AUSTIN BLAIR SIADAK

15

6 OF 30

of the rise in food prices on the global middle classes has meant a shift away from medical care and certain non-essential items such as clothing. For those living on $2 a day, it means cutting out meat from their diets and removing children from school. For those on $1 a day, it means removing meat and vegetables and eating only cereals. And for those living on 50 cents a day, in Sheeran's words, "it means total disaster."[17] Thus, for the poorest of the poor, recent price increases pose serious threats to food security as well as dietary and overall health, with numerous negative effects in the short and long term. Worse, the World Bank estimated earlier this year that an additional 100 million people are likely to be pushed into poverty and face food insecurity as a direct result of the food crisis.[18]

As if this were not bad enough for the world's most destitute, the international agencies responsible for feeding and helping them now face problems of titanic magnitudes as they try to cope with dramatic price increases. For organizations providing food assistance, rising prices have translated into enormous budget shortfalls. The WFP, responsible for feeding nearly 90 million people worldwide, first sounded the alarms in late March by saying that it needed $500 million in emergency funding before May 1 or it would have to start cutting rations, and then raised its initial estimate to over $750 million by late April.[19,20] Additionally, the United States Agency for International Development (USAID), which is responsible for dispersing a large portion of federal foreign assistance, said in April that its commodity expenses had increased by 41 percent in the previous six months, creating budgetary pressures in some areas.[21] Though the WFP has since received sufficient funding to avoid any imminent catastrophes, and recently announced a new $1.2 billion assistance package to 62 countries, it will need continued increases in funding to deal with high food costs in the long term.[22] Likewise, unless other development agencies receive more funding immediately and can establish larger budget inflows in the long term, multiple humanitarian disasters could be in store for the future.

Just as the effects of high food prices differ at the household level, some countries have been hit harder than others. In general, developed countries have seen lower price increases than developing countries and net food exporters have been better off than net food importers. While some politicians in developed states such as those in the European Union or United States have begun to clamor for more attention on the issue of high food prices, they have not experienced anything even remotely resembling what is happening in other countries across the globe. For example, food prices in the United States are only expected to increase by four to five percent in 2008, Americans have a much larger variety of food types to substitute for expensive products, and even the greatest price increases in popular foods such as milk and white bread have been a (relatively) modest 23 and 16 percent respectively.[23] Needless to say, such events seem miniscule when compared to what has happened in Haiti or Cameroon, where violent protests over food and fuel costs in February 2008 led to the deaths of at least 40 people.[24] In Egypt, a doubling of staple food prices in recent months earlier this year led to protests that resulted in the shooting of a young boy.[25] Similarly, large price increases and disorderly events have occurred in the Philippines, Mozambique, Pakistan, and Indonesia, among others. Overall, net food exporters such as the United States and Australia have gained the most from terms of trade improvements, while net importers such as most African and some south Asian states, as well as many non-oil producing Middle Eastern countries have faced larger budget deficits.[26] The interesting, and telling, point is that those places that have been the most affected, and where the most violent reactions have been, are all poor or developing countries that have low per capita incomes, depend heavily on imported food, and/or lack the governmental capacity to contend with volatile price swings. The global food crisis threatens not only the health of the world's poorest people, but also of the world's poorest governments, as will be discussed later.

Not surprisingly, jumps in global food prices have elicited a host of governmental reactions around the globe, especially in those states that have been hit hardest. In order to placate nervous consumers and ensure sufficient domestic food stockpiles, numerous developing countries have imposed price controls, prohibited exports of certain crops, or increased subsidies. In India, the government has effectively banned exports of all non-basmati rice, as well as the export of milk powder products; China has banned all rice and maize exports and increased subsidies to farmers; the Philippines government has even made rice hoarding punishable by death. In addition, Vietnam recently reduced rice exports by a fifth, Bolivia banned export of soy oil to numerous South American states, and Ethiopia banned the export of major cereal crops. Other countries, such as Morocco and Nigeria, have reduced tariffs and other restrictions on imports in an attempt to lower the price of imported food as much as possible.[27,28] Some states have shown strong initiative in tackling the crisis responsibly by increasing cash transfer programs for their citizens and expanding social safety nets, but so far such important actions have not been scaled up to the level necessary to stop many of the poor from slipping through the cracks.[29]

International organizations have also responded loudly, if stopping short of taking all the necessary steps to stem the crisis. Following the lead of organizations such as the WFP that began calling for greater attention months ago, UN Secretary General Ban Ki-moon released a statement in April 2008 saying that the United Nations and World Bank would jointly establish a task force to address the problems created by the food crisis, especially concerning its effects on impoverished regions and peoples.[30] World Bank President Robert Zoellick termed the plan a "New Deal for Global Food Policy."[31] Both men emphatically encouraged states to provide the nearly $1 billion in emergency relief spending that organizations such as the WFP needed immediately to continue operations, with Ban stating, "Without full funding of these emergency requirements, we risk again the specter of widespread hunger, malnutrition, and social unrest on an unprecedented scale." Zoellick and Ban also discouraged the widespread use of export bans because they "encourage hoarding, drive up prices and hurt the poorest people around the world who are struggling to feed themselves."[32] Since then, at least two major international meetings have taken place to discuss the crisis, most prominently the UN "Conference on World Food Security: Challenges of Climate Change and Bioenergy" held in June 2008 in Rome. At this meeting, Ban called for a 50 percent increase in global food output by 2030 and, together with other development heads, voiced the need for a "second green revolution."[33] While these high level summits have notably called for a refocusing of attention on small farmers in developing countries, governments have stuck hard to their differing national interests and little consensus has been made on important issues, including the essential task of delineating which actors will be responsible for the implementation of proposed policy actions.[34]

Reponses have come more slowly in the United States and Europe, but governments in both have expressed strong desires to help stop the current crisis. Largely because gains in food prices have been more gradual and moderate in the U.S. than in most other nations around the world, there has been little public backlash over the issue and few politicians have made much of it. Still, action has begun to be taken as the costs of the global food crisis have started to filter into the American economy in tangible ways, and multiple U.S. Senate hearings have been called to address the issue both in the United States and around the rest of the world as well.[35] Last April, President Bush freed up over $200 million in food aid and called on Congress to approve an extra $770 million dollars in food aid and related measures in order to "[send] a clear message to the world that America will lead the fight against hunger for years to come."[36] Across the pond, state and European Union government officials have agreed that they must help in financing solutions to the current crisis and in establishing greater global food security, yet EU politicians appear apprehensive to seriously consider restructuring policies such as the multi-billion dollar Common Agricultural Policy (CAP) that supplies enormous food subsidies to European farmers and, while perhaps not directly causing current problems, certainly does not aid in their solutions.[37]

Despite the destructive effects that high food prices have caused throughout the world, there are some actors who may not mind if solutions take time to gestate. In any crisis there are both losers and winners, and the easiest winners to see in the current crisis are farmers in developed countries. While their counterparts in poor nations face problems in procuring basic food items for their families, cannot pay the rising costs of yield-increasing fertilizers, must sell at lower prices because they can not store their harvests, and generally lack advanced agricultural technologies, farmers in developed countries are experiencing the greatest boom their sector has seen in decades. As farmer Erwin Johnson of Charles City, Iowa told the *Washington Post*, "This is a fantastic time to be farming. I'm 65, but I can't quit now."[38] His enthusiasm is understandable: for his corn, Johnson currently receives more than twice as much as he did just a couple of years ago.[39] With corn, wheat, soybeans, alfalfa, and most other crops fetching prices double or triple what they did just a few years ago, many farmers in rich countries have seen their incomes increase by twofold or more and can afford the more expensive fertilizer costs and modest gains in food prices.

Though farmers are those benefiting most visibly, they are not the only ones winning and are not even those profiting most. Others like Erwin Johnson currently sell their crops for top dollar, but they will not actually see the money until their next harvest. The reason? Most farmers have already sold their crops from last year's harvest and at last year's prices, meaning that they are not gaining much at this moment while prices shoot higher. Those who appear to be winning the most from the global food crisis are the commodities traders who buy the crops from farmers and sell them on the global market, as well as firms that provide farming equipment and financial speculators betting on future global food prices. The two largest global food traders, Cargill Incorporated and Archer Daniels Midland Company (ADM), reported 2007 profits up a combined 103 percent from the year before, and food giant The Monsanto Company saw profits in the third quarter more than double. Deere and Company, famous for its tractors, experienced a 55 percent rise in profit in the same time period, and The Mosaic Company, one of the world's largest fertilizer manufactures, increased its third quarter net income nearly 12 fold.[40] Concerning speculation, the *International Herald Tribune* reported in April that "On the Chicago CME Group market, which deals in some 25 agricultural commodities...the volume of contracts has increased by 20 percent since the start of the year and now has reached the level of a million contracts a day. This will soon exceed the rate of growth reached in all of 2007."[41] Of course, not every one of these contracts will bring a profit for their owners, but a large number will, and at such high trading volume, some will make a fortune.

In sum, cheap food prices, which prevailed for the past few decades, have become a thing of the past as food prices for the world's most popular crops doubled, tripled, and even quadrupled in the past six to 12 months. Those left worst off by these price jumps are the world's poor, who already have trouble buying enough food for their families and simply cannot keep up with enormous rises in food prices. Expensive food has pushed the majority of the more than one billion living on less than $1 a day deeper into poverty, while welcoming tens of millions more into that category. Those in developed countries also feel the pinch, but they have many more options than do the poor and have not been as harshly affected. Developing countries have been hit hardest, cementing the fact that this is a crisis that most affects both poor people and poor countries, and have responded with a variety of drastic measures to keep food at home or import it more cheaply from abroad. Both international organizations and developed countries recognize their responsibility in bringing the situation under control and have demonstrated a desire to help prevent possible disasters, but have failed to take necessary steps toward fixing long term problems. In the meantime, farmers in

*The Economist* notes, "what is most remarkable about the present [food crisis] is that record prices are being achieved at a time not of scarcity but of abundance. ... [T]his year's total cereals crop will be 1.66 billion tonnes, the largest on record and 89m tonnes more than last year's harvest, another bumper crop."

developed countries, as well as financial speculators and commodity traders, are profiting nicely. That is the current state of the global food crisis. The real question though is how it will be solved. Before that can be addressed, however, another question must first be must answered: what caused the crisis?

Not Your Grandfather's Food Crisis

One of the most interesting aspects of the current food crisis is how different its causes are from those of traditional episodes of starvation and famine. In the past, food shortages largely occurred in relatively concentrated areas, usually as a result of drought, crop failure, population pressures, or war. While some of these have played a role in creating current problems, there exist other factors that make this new crisis very different. Not only has it spread globally, it is a product of global events, helped by the globalization and liberalization of food markets worldwide. Moreover, the current crisis is happening not at a time of global crop failure and dwindling supply, but rather one of record harvests. Four factors in particular have been most prominently cited as the principle causes of the current crisis: Weather-related crop failures possibly due to advancing climate change, a steady upward pressure on demand as a result of larger incomes in developing countries, high oil and fertilizer prices, and increased production of biofuels.

The recent rise in food prices would be easy to understand if it were simply a matter of crop failures and food shortages. This is how famines have played out throughout history, from the Irish Potato Famine to many supply disruptions in poor countries around the world. As predictions and realizations about changing weather patterns due to climate change worsen, it also would not be a large surprise if rising temperatures and drought were to destroy crops and ruin harvests around the globe. Some say it has even begun to happen: In Australia, one of the world's largest producers and exporters of grain, the wheat crop has failed for two years in a row and prospects do not look good for the coming harvest.[42] Moreover, global wheat supply has been outpaced by demand for seven of the last eight years.[43] Perhaps high food prices are just a product of crop failures and food shortages.

However, while some crops have failed around the world, this argument fails to hold for a number of reasons. First, as *The Economist* notes, "what is most remarkable about the present [food crisis] is that record prices are being achieved at a time not of scarcity but of abundance. ... [T]his year's total cereals crop will be 1.66 billion tonnes, the largest on record and 89m tonnes more than last year's harvest, another bumper crop."[44] Though some isolated failed harvests exist, it does not change the fact that global food production is at an all time high. Moreover, even if crops fail in one area, the globalization of the food market makes it possible, in theory, to import needed grains or staple crops. Thus, Australia's woes will not make it unable to feed its people, though it may cost more to do so.

The more fundamental problem, rather, has been where the current supply of food is being directed. Some countries are net producers and exporters of food, while others consistently import large percentages of their food supply, and in the past year many of the net exporters have attempted to keep prices down within their own borders by limiting the export of certain crops. Such events have happened in nearly all major food commodities markets, most notably in the rice market, and over 30 countries world wide currently have some form of export ban in place.[45] Unfortunately, this creates an extremely distorted market where supplies do not flow to areas where demand is the highest, creating severe shortages and raising food prices for those countries not fortunate enough to be net producers themselves. Thus, though supply problems may have been behind many famous famines and food crises, and a string of current supply shortages in certain places around the world certainly do not help bring prices down, they are not the major cause of the current crisis. Rather, the fact that prices have risen so dramatically even at a time of bumper crops can only signify one thing: an enormous increase in demand.

It is simple economics: when the demand for a good increases, so does its price. Globally, the demand for food is growing at an enormous rate and is one of the main drivers behind higher prices. Unprecedented economic growth in many developing countries has increased the purchasing power of their consumers, translating into a huge rise in demand for non-staple foods that were once unattainable, such as beef. *The New York Times* reports, "As the newly urbanized and newly affluent seek more protein and more calories, a phenomenon called 'diet globalization' is playing out around the world. Demand is growing for pork in Russia, beef in Indonesia and dairy products in Mexico. Rice is giving way to noodles, home-cooked food to fast food."[46] In China, where growth has been phenomenal and over 300 million people have been brought out of poverty in recent decades, the average consumption of meat per capita in 1980 was only 20 kilograms. Today it is 55 kilograms. Given that growing cattle takes an extraordinary amount

of both grain and water – 150 to 250 gallons of water to produce a pound of wheat, and seven to nine pounds of wheat to produce one pound of beef – the demand increase in China alone takes an enormous toll on the world's resources.[47] And it is not just meat that is becoming more common. As one Nigerian explains, bread in his country (which often uses expensive imported grain in production) is no longer a delicacy, but a staple: "The moment you develop a taste, you are hooked."[48] When one sees events such as those in China and Nigeria play out across the world, greatly increasing world demand, high global food prices become much easier to understand.

However, the global increase in demand for non-staple foods has been a slow and steady process playing out over decades, and a simple supply/demand explanation alone cannot account for the rapid price increases seen in the past few months. Enter our third culprit: high oil prices. It is no secret that oil prices have skyrocketed to new highs in 2008, reaching $116.27 per barrel for light crude as of August 27th (down from highs near $150 per barrel earlier in the summer) from less than $30 a barrel in 2002 and less than $65 a barrel in 2006.[49] High fuel prices, in turn, raise the price of food in two major ways. First, higher oil prices mean higher transportation and energy costs, which translate into higher food prices because most food grown around the world travels at least some distance from producer to consumer, many times crossing international borders en route, and any method of transportation from truck, to rail, to boat, or plane requires oil. For example, when a shipping company has to pay more for fuel to ship a boatload of wheat from the U.S. to Nigeria, it cannot absorb all of the costs itself and must pass them on to the consumer in the form of higher prices. In addition, most farmers in developed countries rely heavily on large tractors to plant and bring in their harvests, and high fuel costs add to the costs of producing their food as well. In other areas of the supply chain, such as storage facilities and local distribution, higher energy prices across the board lead to more expensive food.

Second, the gross majority of fertilizers used by all farmers in developed countries and many of the farmers in developing countries are petroleum based, meaning that their prices increase with the price of oil. In addition, between

1996 and 2008, there was a 36 percent global increase in the demand for fertilizers and a 56 percent increase in developing countries alone, largely due to an increase in crop production to fill the growing food demand around the world. However, fertilizer producers have not kept up, leading to large shortages of fertilizer on the global market. This growing gap between supply and demand, combined with an increase in the price of oil used to make fertilizers, has caused the price of some fertilizers to triple and the price of nearly all types to rise significantly.[50] This presents an enormous cost increase to farmers whose crops depend on these fertilizers, and just as shipping firms must pass on the cost of transportation to consumers, so too must farmers pass on the rising costs of fertilizers in the form of higher food prices. In the face of expensive fertilizers, some farmers have begun to replace chemical based fertilizers with traditional methods such as pig manure, but such techniques result in reduced crop yields and only increase the growing difference between global food supply and demand.

The final factor mentioned as one of the main causes of the current crisis is the recent increase in the demand for biofuels, such as ethanol and biodiesel. It may at first appear paradoxical that an outcome of the well-intentioned global environmental movement could negatively affect the world's poor, but a closer look at the current production of biofuels makes it clear. Recall that the current food crisis does not stem from a traditional supply shortage, but rather a problem of where the current supply is being directed. The basic problem with biofuels is that they increase these supply disruptions, diverting a large percentage of certain crops toward fuel production and away from hungry mouths. In 2008, for example, between one-fifth and one-quarter of the U.S. corn crop went toward ethanol production, resulting in a wide range of negative cascading effects.[51] First, and most plainly, there is less corn to go around, causing the price of corn and all corn-based products to increase dramatically. For example, corn is a popular ingredient of animal feed, and high corn prices have in turn raised the price of meat.[52] Second, farmers know there is a huge demand for corn and have substituted it for other food crops, such as wheat or soybeans, reducing the supply of these crops and pushing up their market prices as well. Third, it results in a further linking of fuel and food prices: Because biofuels are oil's major substitute, their price is inherently tied to the price of oil. Therefore, when oil prices increase, so do biofuel prices, leading to an increased willingness of farmers to supply the corn and other crops used in making biofuels, and raising corn prices as well as the price of many other grains and crops.[53] In addition, high grain prices greatly increase the value of land, leading in some places to harmful deforestation as previously forested areas are cleared to make room for corn, soy, or other crops. While biofuels proponents discount claims that they have had much of a negative impact on food prices, a recent study by the IFPRI estimated that, by injecting a huge new demand increase into the global market and taking more grains away from food production between 2000 and 2007, biofuels were responsible for a 30 percent increase in the price of grains as a whole.[54]

## IN 2008, FOR EXAMPLE, BETWEEN ONE-FIFTH AND ONE-QUARTER OF THE U.S. CORN CROP WENT TOWARD ETHANOL PRODUCTION.

Though each of the preceding explanations plays a large role in raising food prices, there are a few more fundamental, if less often reported, factors at play. The first concerns global reserves and stockpiles of grains and other staple crops. While global food supply is at record levels, stockpiles are not. As a result of increasing market liberalization over the past few decades, "... the once-common practice of hoarding grains to protect against the kind of shortfall the world is seeing now seemed more and more archaic," reports the *Washington Post*.[55] The effect was a global reduction in grain reserves that did not seem to pose much of a problem, and

DISCOURSE

THE FORGOTTEN CRISIS
HOW HIGH FOOD PRICES HAVE
IMPOVERISHED MILLIONS AND
THREATENED GOVERNMENTS

AUSTIN BLAIR SIADAK

21

12 OF 30

made food even cheaper. Now, however, as demand greatly outstrips supply, governments around the world have dipped into their reserves to fill the gap, running their stockpiles of staple crops down to record lows in attempts to feed their people and keep the price of food from shooting even higher. One commodity analysis firm reports that global grain reserves have fallen from an average of 114.7 days of use in 1990-2000 to only 56.7 days of use last year.[56] These actions subsequently resulted in higher food prices as market traders and speculators began to realize that some governments would not be able to feed their populations, or would have to pay dearly in order to do so, and raised their bets on food futures, in turn raising current prices.

Trading and speculation appear to be another major cause of the current crisis in their own right. In the past, before trading of commodities reached the levels that it has today, if a government were to run down its reserves it could still keep the price of food under control because food prices were not determined at the global level. Today however, this is nearly impossible due to the globalized nature of the food market. A large majority of the world's crops are bought and sold at major commodities markets in Chicago, Minneapolis, and Kansas City, and world prices are determined in the pits as brokers buy and sell spot and future exchanges of wheat, maize, soybeans, and all kinds of foods. Government purchases also play a large role in determining price.[57]

When food prices began to rise last summer, speculators and traders dove headfirst into the action. Due to the downturn of the stock market following the growing mortgage crisis in the United States, many investors were looking for a new place to invest and threw hundreds of millions of dollars into grains futures. Many say that this caused a quick rise in the price of grains and a subsequent increase in the price of food, though others are wary of this explanation and say that increased speculation is just as much a symptom of the current crisis as it is a cause.[58] Still, says David King, Secretary-General of the International Federation of Agricultural Producers, "Even if it is difficult to gauge the real impact of this financial speculation, it has certainly played a role in influencing trading prices."[59] William Pfaff of the *International Herald Tribune* notes that

"Speculative purchases have no other purpose than to make money for the speculators, who hold their contracts to drive up current prices with the intention not of selling the commodities on the real future market, but of unloading their holdings onto an artificially inflated market, at the expense of the ultimate consumer."[60] It is important to realize, though, that future contracts in the food market themselves are not a bad things, as they have "classically have been the means by which a limited number of traders stabilized future commodity prices and enabled farmers to finance themselves through future sales."[61] What is worrisome is that more and more untraditional "non-commercial" speculators, traders, and hedge funds have come to see the food market as a place first and foremost to make a profit. Regardless of speculation's role in causing high prices, there are new fears that it is causing prices to lie about current supply and demand, creating the possibility of a growing agricultural bubble that could prove disastrous for both farmers and consumers.[62] In the end, most involved in the market admit that, at the very least, without this recent influx of speculation prices would be lower than they are today.[63]

Another extremely important cause is the rash string of export bans and other actions that some governments took last year and in the beginning of this year in their early attempts to stem the rise in food prices. Near the end of 2007, with global food prices rising, speculation sending futures ever higher, and food riots beginning to flare up across the world, many governments started placing orders in the commodities market for enormous quantities of food. The weak dollar made the U.S. market appear enticing, and as the *Washington Post* reports, "They put in orders on U.S. grain exchanges two to three times larger than normal...[leading] major domestic U.S. mills to jump into the fray with their own massive orders, fearing that there would soon be no wheat left at any price."[64] These runs on global harvests caused speculators to bet futures higher and sent the price of staple foods upward. In addition, the institution of export bans and other methods of food hoarding by government around the globe caused prices to accelerate quickly early this year. The reason is that these actions contribute to supply misdirection and create market distortions by artificially reducing the supply of tradable food and increasing market volatility, causing prices to rise and speculators to bet up futures prices.

Finally, the devaluation of the dollar in recent years caused food prices to rise as well. Because many international exchanges of grains and other crops are denominated in U.S. dollars, even if food prices had remained unchanged over the past few years in terms of other currencies their market price would still have risen. However, prices across the board have not stayed steady during this time period, adding to the price increases due to devaluation alone. The IFPRI estimated earlier this year that the role played by the dropping value of the dollar alone could amount to anywhere between a 15 and 27 percent increase in the rise of food prices in the past two years.[65]

To summarize, the current food crisis was not caused just by one or two factors, but by a confluence of events that combined to send food prices through the roof. Though traditional food shortages often arise out of supply shortages, the current crisis has been caused by a large supply that has simply not kept up with an even larger demand. The global increase in demand for resource intensive foods over the past few decades has put a large strain on food production, but its slow nature means that it alone cannot explain the rapid increase in prices. Rather, this swift price jump came from a combination of high transportation and fertilizer costs due to rising oil prices, as well as a shift of some crops away from food production to satisfy a new demand in the market for biofuels and ethanol. In addition, as demand outpaced supply and prices moved upward countries depleted their grain reserves, leading commodities traders and speculators to bet prices even higher. The final push was caused by export bans and grain hoarding around the world, as well as a run on American grain markets in the end of 2007 and beginning of 2008 as governments feared a looming shortage and attempted to buy as much grain as possible. Viewing these actions, speculators and traders further increased their predictions for food futures, resulting in unprecedented global food prices at the end of April and into early summer.

An interesting point that these causes make clear is that they are almost all a by-product of the linking of the global food chain that has occurred in the past decades. From field to shelf the world's food now runs through multiple countries and exchanges numerous hands. Farmers in one country grow food for hungry mouths in another, selling it to large commodity traders who in turn place it in global exchange markets where prices are largely determined by traders and speculators. Policies in one country, such as strict control of oil supply by Middle Eastern states or export bans of certain crops in developing countries, can have far reaching effects on the food security of the rest of the world, and even well intentioned policies such as U.S. ethanol mandates can produce a host of negative effects. Theoretically, the benefit of such a system is that even when problems do develop, such as the current crisis, the participation of numerous nations will hopefully create more avenues for success; if one country fails to produce enough food for its people, the global market should allow it to easily avoid massive starvation by purchasing abroad. However, if countries fail to work together it means a worsening of the crisis as they fight between each other over a commodity more precious than any other. Given this situation, what does the future hold in the short and medium term concerning the global food crisis, and how can it best be resolved?

What Is In Store?

While it is difficult to predict what will happen in the coming months and years, especially given the varied nature of both the causes and effects of the current crisis, there are a number of short and medium term effects that are quite likely. The first, and most important, is that high food prices are here to stay for quite some time. We can understand this just by looking back at the four most widely cited causes of the crisis: Prices could most easily go down if global supply were to quickly catch up with and surpass global demand, if demand were to drop enough for the current supply to suffice, if oil and fertilizer prices dropped significantly, or if biofuels demands decreased dramatically. None of these scenarios is going to play out anytime soon. Let's look at each in turn.

Greatly increasing global food supply would be one of the best ways to counter the current food crisis, as it would cause prices and speculation to rapidly drop and avoid multiple humanitarian catastrophes. Unfortunately, this will not happen quickly because supply can only go up by bringing more land under cultivation or increasing yields, neither of which can have an effect in the short run. Concerning the first, one of the upsides of high prices is that they give incentives to farmers to plant new crops and produce at an all-out pace, which will eventually increase supply. Still, even when farmers decide to produce more wheat, corn, or soy, it usually takes a year or more for their decisions to come to fruition as fields need to be sown, crops planted, and harvests collected.[66] Thus, in economic terms food supply is rather "sticky," and a ten percent increase in prices generally only leads to a one to two percent increase in supply, according to the IFPRI.[67] Additionally, though there is a lot of unused land around the world which could be brought into agricultural production, as *The Economist* states, "much of the new land is in remote parts of Brazil, Russia, Kazakhstan, the Congo and Sudan: it would require big investments in roads and other infrastructure, which could take decades – and would often lead to the clearing of precious forest."[68] Lastly, bringing new land under cultivation will become more and more difficult as rapid urbanization continues to sweep the globe, burying valuable land underneath parking lots and apartment buildings.

Increasing yields in the short term is also problematic. Ideally, a farmer who wants to get more bang for his buck could simply plant new and improved seed varieties for the next year's harvest, but this is only possible if research and development have been going into new seeds and crops. Unfortunately, as the last century drew to a close, low food prices and the lack of any significant supply shortages since the 1970s caused governments and companies to relax investment in the development of new crops. This was especially prevalent in the developing world where many governments seem to have thought their agricultural problems fixed after the Green Revolution. The result is a world that currently lacks any significantly improved staple crop seeds, and developing them could take anywhere from ten to 15 years, says Bob Zeigler of the International Rice Research Institute (IRRI) in the Philippines.[69] Increasing investments in machinery and fertilizers can help in the meantime, but they alone will not be able to dramatically improve yields or supply in the next few months or even the next few years.

What about the demand side of the equation? It is extremely unlikely that global food demand will decrease in the short term given its constant upward pressure for decades. Global population growth shows no signs of slowing any time soon, and the great majority of those born in the next few decades will be born in poor and developing states where diets are changing the most.[70] Reduced economic growth worldwide could possibly do the trick, and it certainly seems that the global economy is currently entering a downturn, but many nations have still been prospering as of late and it would take a multitude of catastrophic events for all developing countries to stop growing (moreover, while lower growth rates would reduce food demand they would also usher in a host of other economic and social problems that the world certainly does not want to see). Thus, it seems certain that even more global citizens will demand better diets in the future and that we are still on the upward slope of the curve. As Daniel W. Basse of the agricultural consultancy firm AgResource Company ominously told the *New York Times* in April, "'Everyone wants to eat like an American on this globe. But if they do, we're going to need another two or three globes to grow it all.'"[71]

High oil prices are also likely to continue for the foreseeable future, keeping transportation and fertilizer costs high as well. There has not been a significant reduction in oil prices, which would need to happen for transportation to become cheaper, since the 1990s and worries about peak oil and dwindling supply will probably send the price even higher. Fertilizer prices will hopefully drop somewhat in the next few years as more production sites are created (there are currently 50 under construction worldwide) and as supply catches up with demand.[72] Still, this will take years, and even when they are finished problems will remain. The use of chemical fertilizers greatly boosts crop yields but often leads to pollution in the form nitrogen runoff, creating "dead sea" zones that kill off local marine wildlife and ecosystems. Despite these negative side-effects they still, however, present humanity's best chance of keeping yields high and avoiding large supply problems, argues Norman

Borlaug, a leading scientist behind the Green Revolution and 1970 Nobel Peace Prize winner: "Without chemical fertilizer, forget it. The game is over."[73]

It is too early right now to determine exactly what the future holds for biofuels production and mandates in the United States and the rest of the world, but it appears that they are here to stay as well. On the one hand there was fierce support for the introduction of the mandates into last year's U.S. energy bill, and on the other there are increasing realizations that ethanol may actually be harming the world more than it helps. Even Secretary of State Condoleeza Rice recently noted the possible negative effects of biofuels on global food prices, but the Bush administration is still standing strong behind its current policy for the time being.[74] The world would benefit from a reduction in biofuels mandates, as will be explained later, but high oil prices will continue to make "sustainable" fuels such as ethanol appear as relatively easy and cheap solutions. At the very least, any change in current policy will not come immediately and it will take time for the political opposition to biofuels to be built, especially so soon after many in Washington felt hard pressed to put ethanol mandates into law. [75]

The other factors do not offer much hope either. Global grain reserves are only going to increase if supply runs higher than demand or if governments decide to stockpile and not distribute what they buy. We have already seen that the first option will not happen soon, and though some governments have begun to hoard food within their own borders it is unlikely that they will choose not to give it to their citizens for fear of social unrest and violent uprisings. Unfortunately, continued low reserves will probably keep speculators active for the time being. Speculation itself is not likely to stop any time soon, bar a large scale intervention by government authorities around the world to reign in some of the more egregious actors. Even this is improbable in the short term given the gap between the political capital necessary for such action and the lack of a widespread call for intervention. Lastly, governments around the world interested in keeping the peace at home are likely to continue buying large amounts of food at a time from exporters as well as instituting export bans and other harmful measures.

Though these actions worsen the problem at the global level, governments do not want to be left without enough food for their people and care more about the immediate effects of the crisis at home than those felt around the rest of the world. There is some hope that an appreciating dollar could bring prices down somewhat, but its value would have to rise quite a bit to have any sort of large effect on global prices. All in all, these factors will combine to keep food prices very high in 2008 and 2009, and prices for most crops will remain above 2004 levels until at least 2015.[76]

High food prices will also continue to be unequal in their effects on the world's population. The poor are undoubtedly those who face the greatest risks, but high prices will not affect all poor people in the same way. Those most at risk will continue to be the absolute poor who rely on international or state handouts, because higher food prices for them truly mean the difference between life and death. Severe malnutrition will be stark realities for many of these people, of whom there are hundreds of millions on the planet. Beyond the ultra-poor, the major divides both at the national and household levels will be between net sellers and net buyers of food, as well as between rural and urban populations. Overall, net sellers and exporters will benefit more than buyers and importers because they receive higher prices for their products and at the national level do not have to buy food at high international prices. This may be good news for a large rice exporter like Thailand, but is a nightmare for extremely poor net importers such as Indonesia or Niger.[77,78] Urban populations will tend to be worse off because they do not produce their own food and are thus net food buyers, though this effect could be somewhat mitigated by higher incomes in urban areas. One must be careful, however, in not supposing that all rural populations and farmers will benefit from the current crisis. While the World Bank reports that over 80 percent of the three billion people living in rural areas in developing countries are involved in farming in some capacity, and thus might be expected to benefit from high food prices, in reality most of these farmers own very small plots of land and are not net sellers of food. Even for those who are, the size of price jumps often outweighs increases in prices they receive for their crops due to imperfect information flows and other market externalities.[79] One must

DISCOURSE

THE FORGOTTEN CRISIS
HOW HIGH FOOD PRICES HAVE
IMPOVERISHED MILLIONS AND
THREATENED GOVERNMENTS

AUSTIN BLAIR SIADAK

25

16 OF 30

also be careful not to think that all poor countries will face similar problems due to urban poverty, because some have much larger urban populations than others – the urban poor constitute half of all poor people in Bolivia, while less than a tenth in Vietnam and Cambodia.[80] Overall, though, those places likely to suffer the most are poor countries that are both net importers of food and have large numbers of urban poor. The effects of the crisis are likely to be smaller on poor populations who rely heavily on local food crops, such as potatoes in the Andes or teff in Ethiopia, rather than those traded internationally because their price and supply are not determined at the global level.[81]

Development programs and plans for poverty reduction around the world will also face immense difficulties as high food prices affect the health and purchasing power of the world's poor. As already noted, the estimated 100 million people worldwide that have been pushed into poverty due to increased food prices significantly negates many of the gains made in poverty reduction in recent decades. Moreover, according to a recent IFPRI report, "the poor... [get] the vast majority of their caloric intake from staple crops and [consume] very little in the way of... [foods] which are rich in essential micronutrients.... [As] prices continue to rise, the poor will experience a worsening of dietary quality...and the very poor will also experience decreased caloric intake."[82] One large fear is the effects that deteriorating diets will have on pregnant women, their offspring, and preschool aged children, all of who need proper nutrition to avoid severe health problems in the short and long term.[83]

Furthermore, the problems will spread beyond just malnutrition and starvation. Due to decreased purchasing power, some poor will remove their children from school in order to work, especially girls, taking from future generations one of their best hopes for escaping poverty. Others may prioritize food above other extremely important areas, such as proper healthcare and immunizations, increasing levels of debilitating diseases in developing countries. Even worse, in order to buy any food at all, many of the world's poor are selling everything they have, including their tools, livestock, and other assets, meaning that recovery, when it comes, will be much more difficult.[84] Development in any field, be it education, health, economics, or politics, will simply not happen if people are not healthy and getting enough food to eat, and thus no development program will remain untouched by the current crisis. To take one prominent example, it may be fair to say that the current food crisis will be the final nail in the coffin of achieving the UN's Millennium Development Goals, the first of which alone (to cut in half the percentage of those suffering from hunger and extreme poverty between 1990 and 2015) looks dimmer and dimmer as the effects of the food crisis become more clear.

Another likely problem is that insecurity and unrest will increase in weak and developing states as food prices fail to go down and their citizens become more desperate. Already food riots have spread throughout the world as prices exceed people's ability to pay, seen in the examples of Haiti, Cameroon, and Egypt mentioned earlier. The reason poor states are most likely to experience increased rioting and state insecurity is due to a variety of factors. The main problem is that they contain more poor people who are having the hardest time dealing with high food prices. Thus, theirs is the daunting task of avoiding starvation and providing food for those who simply cannot afford enough, in addition to dealing with the negative health and developmental effects of malnutrition and decreased purchasing power among the poor. In comparison, developed states need not worry much about such matters. Furthermore, poor states often lack the institutional and governmental capability to solve these severe problems, and it is probable that at least some will be unable to satisfy their citizens' demands for cheaper food. In these states the likely result will be greater social discontent because, quite frankly, when people cannot eat they get angry. Given that many poor countries also lack strong traditions of non-violent dispute resolution or have recently experienced conflicts, and combined with the fact that the majority of the world's poor have no idea of why prices have risen so much recently and often see the state as the cause of their problems, violent clashes appear in store for some poor and weak states.

The above effects will be magnified by the fact that increasing food costs will create budgetary problems for many poor states, even if they do not face large security threats. *The Economist* reported earlier this year that developing countries will pay $50 billion to import cereals alone in 2008, up ten percent from last year. Though a few hundred million is not a big concern to most developed states, it can be a large percentage of most developing countries' budgets. Mauritania, for example, imports 70 percent of the food that its people eat, costing over ten percent of total GDP, and its import expenditures are expected to rise by tens of millions of dollars over the costs of just a few years ago.[85] Costs are rising in other areas as well. In India the government's fertilizer subsidies which cost only $4 billion in 2004-2005 are expected to run up to $22 billion this year, an increase of over 400 percent.[86] The problem for these poor countries is that they must try to provide enough food for their people or face significant public backlash, and as the costs of feeding their populations continue to rise many may have to make hard decisions about shifting funds away from other government projects, such as investments in infrastructure, transportation, or education. One example can be seen in how many poor states, such as Egypt and Pakistan, are currently trying to avoid violence and insecurity by increasing food handouts, subsidies, and other social protection programs.[87] While these policies depress prices and quell problems in the short term, they can only last so long before cutting into the budgets of other projects. If other solutions are not found soon such actions could have a variety of negative consequences further down the road as vital sectors of societies and economies do not get the attention they need.

One possible effect that has not materialized strongly yet, but shows signs of happening, is an increase in negative perceptions of market liberalization across the globe. Despite the beneficial effects that globalization has had for the global economy in the past few decades, attitudes toward globalization have been increasingly negative in recent years in many developed and developing countries, and it will be very difficult for the proponents of liberalization to argue that the globalization of the food market did not play a large role in facilitating the current crisis.[88] While most newspaper articles and analyses of the crisis originally just touched on the first four factors mentioned earlier as causes of the

DISCOURSE
THE FORGOTTEN CRISIS
HOW HIGH FOOD PRICES HAVE
IMPOVERISHED MILLIONS AND
THREATENED GOVERNMENTS

AUSTIN BLAIR SIADAK

27

18 OF 30

Insecurity and conflict may become more likely in poor states without the resources to feed their people or the authority to police them, and many poor countries will face budgetary problems due to high food costs.

crisis, more and more are beginning to mention the possible roll of speculation in raising prices.[89] Many governments and politicians are also voicing louder concern, such as when French Agriculture Minister Michel Barnier stated in April that "We must not leave the vital issue of feeding people to the mercy of market laws and international speculation," and warned against "too much trust in the free market."[90] In developing countries too, as governments try to shift the blame for rising prices away from themselves and towards other factors, liberalization and globalization could become easy prey. It would be unfortunate and shortsighted, though, if a large increase in protectionist attitudes and policies were to come from the world's current food problems, as they often raise prices and rarely have wide reaching benefits.

Though not guaranteed, a whole range of other effects is possible as well. Migration could increase dramatically in areas of the globe where countries that do not have enough food border those that do. One example is already playing out on the Mauritania-Mali border where thousands of Mauritanian men have crossed over to find jobs and food for their starving families back home.[91] This example demonstrates plainly how perceived differences in job and food opportunities do not have to be very large for migration to occur, as both countries are extremely poor. Another possible effect that has received almost no attention is the impact of higher food costs on small and local businesses in poor countries.[92] Employers with just a few employees are likely to find it increasingly difficult to pay their staff as food and energy costs rise, which could spell disaster for the millions of such operations around the globe. One huge question this raises is how the global food crisis is going to affect the ability of tens of millions of micro-credit borrowers in poor states to repay their loans as food prices shoot up, and what effects this may have on the global micro-credit industry. It is possible that loans could help the poor pay for food that they would currently be unable to purchase, helping to mitigate would-be disasters. It is equally likely, though, that many poor people, having borrowed to purchase food, may find themselves unable to pay back loans, causing default rates to increase dramatically and push millions deeper into poverty.

In review, high food prices will remain for many years as global supply slowly catches up with demand. On the supply side, farmers around the world will begin to plant more, more land will be brought into cultivation, and new technologies will be employed, but none of these will make large differences for a few years at the very least. Global demand will increase as the populations of developing countries grow, high oil prices will keep transportation costs expensive, and fertilizer prices will remain high in the short run until current supply shortages are balanced out. Biofuels subsidies are also likely to continue for the time being, which will help keep grain prices high, and it will not help that grain reserves are unlikely to increase at a global level, that market speculation shows no signs of slowing, or that many developing countries with weak bureaucracies see easy relief in deleterious export bans and price controls. In addition, the absolute poor will continue to be the most affected by the crisis, and net food importers and buyers will face large problems while net exporters and sellers gain at both the macroeconomic and household levels. Development programs the world over are likely to experience difficulties as the food crisis filters into their work. Insecurity and conflict may become more likely in poor states without the resources to feed their people or the authority to police them, and many poor countries will face budgetary problems due to high food costs. Protectionist attitudes and policies may become more popular if liberalization and speculation are seen as the major causes of the current crisis, and migration could increase around the world as people move in search of cheaper food. A final worry that must be studied more is the effect of the food crisis on popular micro-credit businesses.

How to Fix the Food Crisis

It should be obvious by now just how large of a problem the global food crisis is. Given its magnitude, it should also be obvious that solving it will not be a quick fix. The goal at this point is to stabilize current prices and work to bring them back down to reasonable levels in coming months and years, in addition to restructuring international food markets and financing efforts to increase global food supply. The global nature of the problem will require international cooperation among governments and a concerted political will to make fundamental changes in global food policy. Changes are also necessary at the personal level as the world comes to grips with the fact that not all humans will be able to eat like Americans, including Americans themselves. I will not try to explain all the possible solutions that should be enacted to fix the food crisis, but will touch on some of the most important and necessary.

First and foremost, the world's rich governments and those countries benefiting from the current crisis must provide the emergency funding needed by humanitarian organizations and poor country governments. The United States should be commended for pledging nearly $1 billion towards alleviating the food crisis, but rhetoric alone will solve nothing. The U.S. and European governments need to stop *saying* that they will provide money and actually start *giving* it to the organizations that need it. Along these lines, Saudi Arabia recently gave the WFP half a *billion* dollars in emergency funding, and the World Bank

DISCOURSE

THE FORGOTTEN CRISIS
HOW HIGH FOOD PRICES HAVE
IMPOVERISHED MILLIONS AND
THREATENED GOVERNMENTS

AUSTIN BLAIR SIADAK

29

20 OF 30

will be doubling agricultural lending to Africa this year to over $800 million.[93] These are the types of actions that are needed to ensure that humanitarian crises will be avoided in the coming months. In addition, as the IFPRI notes, humanitarian agencies are usually good at responding to natural disasters and short term emergencies, but they will need to reform their policies to act more decisively against slow onset disasters like the current one."[94]

Second, harmful biofuels subsidies and mandates should be reexamined and removed both in the United States and Europe due to their negative effects both on the environment and global food prices. Proponents of biofuels say that they are necessary both to improve energy independence and protect the environment. However, given the current ways in which they are produced, neither of these supposed effects is happening. As Indian economist Swaminathan S. Anklesaria Aiyar explains, "Ironically, even if the US and Europe meet their biofuel targets, these will meet only six percent of their transport fuel needs. So, mandated biofuel use cannot give the West independence from Middle East oil supplies."[95] Moreover, a recent study released in the respected journal *Science* found that biofuels production actually creates *more* greenhouse gas emissions than gasoline production – doubling the emissions of gasoline production over 30 years from corn-based ethanol and increasing them 50 percent for biofuels made from switch-grass.[96] Given these facts, and the previously demonstrated ways in which biofuels push up the price of grain, mandates for these supposedly "clean fuels" should either be shifted to only come from waste sources or be scrapped altogether. Doing so could bring up to a twenty percent decrease in the price of maize and a ten percent decrease in the price of wheat, according to the IFPRI.[97]

Third, developing countries must reduce or remove their growing number of export bans and price controls. It is understandable that these countries wish to ensure food security for their citizens, and want to keep food prices down because many of their people are poor and cannot afford expensive food. But export bans and price controls are simply not the best way to achieve this goal. As already mentioned, when a number of countries restrict their grain exports it artificially reduces global supply and needlessly

raises food prices for other countries and consumers who may be even worse off. It could even end up hurting the countries that institute the bans if they need to buy food internationally in the future and will face higher costs due to their own actions.[98] The global food market will work much more effectively if all countries increase their integration instead of further isolating themselves. Price controls are a problem because they artificially depress prices and remove the incentives for farmers to grow more to satisfy raging demand. Though consumers are happy because of cheaper food, failing to increase supply will cause prices to remain high in the long run and will not benefit the billions who depend on small scale farming in developing countries.[99] In addition, blanket price controls benefit both those who need help paying for food as well as those who do not, creating wasteful economic distortions.

Instead, policies should include increasing social protection programs, expanding healthcare, and reducing import restraints. In terms of subsidies, it is better to subsidize poor peoples' incomes rather than food prices because doing so allows states to not only improve incentives for farmers to grow more food and thereby increase rural incomes, but also avoids paying for cheaper food for the rich, all while still allowing the poor to afford food.[100] Also, a wide variety of food and cash transfer programs already exist in many developing countries and these need to be scaled up to deal with the current crisis. In particular, "[they] should target the poorest people, with a focus on early childhood nutrition, regions in distress, school feeding with take-home rations, and food and cash for work," according to a recent IFPRI report.[101] Healthcare and nutrition programs must also be expanded, especially for at-risk groups such as pregnant mothers and young children in order to avoid harmful long term effects of malnutrition. National governments should work to better coordinate funding with humanitarian agencies and implementation with NGOs in this area. Getting rid of import tariffs and restrictions would help by reducing the price of imported food and thereby lowering the costs passed on to consumers. However, any astute reader would be correct to ask how any government could increase social protection programs while reducing tariff revenue, especially in poor states that lack large budgets and efficient bureaucracies. The answer is that these options may require reducing subsidies or expenses in other areas and will not be viable everywhere, because providing income subsidies necessitates a competent civil service that many poor countries lack. Where they are not possible, any price controls should be short-term and directed at certain foods more popular among the poor.[102] Even where such programs are used, any increased food or cash subsidies must be temporary and localized to ensure that consumers do not come to depend on them and to reduce market distortions.[103] Lastly, it is important to note that countries that do not already have social protection programs to scale up will not be able to create them fast enough to do much for the current crisis, and these are the places that will need the most donor assistance in the short term.[104]

Fourth, developed countries must make large changes in their food policies as well. As bad as the current crisis is, it presents an amazing period of opportunity to fix many of the deep-seated problems in the global food market. As the *Washington Post* explains, though trade in food has been globalized and liberalized to a significant degree in recent decades,

-

"[it] never became the kind of well-honed machine that has made the price of manufactured goods such as personal computers and flat-screen TVs increasingly similar worldwide. With food, significant subsidies and other barriers meant to protect farmers...have distorted the real price of food globally, economists say, preventing the market from normal price adjustments as global demand has climbed."[105]

-

While developed countries continued protecting their farmers, a wide range of developing states following recommendations of the "Washington Consensus" in the 1990s reduced price fixing policies and slowed investment in agricultural production, leaving them vulnerable to events like the current crisis.[106] Now, however, as prices head constantly upward and countries around the globe feel the pinch it appears as if there may be enough support and political will to make serious changes in global food trade and policy to fix these imbalances.

The time is ripe to remove or significantly reduce agricultural subsidies to make the global food market more competitive and more just.

Developed countries, predominantly the United States and European nations, should take the current opportunity of high crop prices to remove many of their disastrous agricultural subsidies. The United States currently doles out billions of dollars a year to farmers, and through its Common Agricultural Policy (CAP) the European Union spends over 40 percent of its budget on agricultural subsidies. In addition, the EU has enormously high import tariffs that restrict agricultural imports from many developing countries.[107] Unfortunately these policies result in artificially high incentives to produce in high-cost developed countries, who are often net food exporters as a result, making food imports for poorer countries more expensive during shortages and also making developing country exports less competitive in developed markets.[108] This puts poor farmers in these countries at a disadvantage and discourages growth and development. Now that farmers in developed countries are receiving the highest prices they have seen in decades and will not face severe hardships if subsidies are thrown out, the time is ripe to remove or significantly reduce agricultural subsidies to make the global food market more competitive and more just. These issues should be addressed as part of a larger goal of completing the current Doha round of trade talks.

Fifth, it is also clear that something should be done concerning rampant market volatility and speculation. Decreasing protectionist policies in both developed and developing countries should help remove distortions that are prone to cause wild market swings, but it is less clear as to what exactly should be done to reduce the negative effects of speculation. In addition to causing global food prices to rise faster than they might otherwise, extensive speculation on grain futures leaves many farmers less certain about their contracts and more vulnerable to large losses. Some farmers who have lost faith in traditional organizations such as the Chicago Board of Trade to provide financial security have started to enter into contracts with private financial firms, which provide them with more security but also make tallying the total market supply more difficult, a factor that could make prices even more volatile. While many blame rocky markets on the huge investments in commodities from hedge funds, and see limiting their involvement as a possible solution, hedge fund capital adds liquidity to the market and should theoretically make prices less volatile.[109] For the time being no one knows exactly how to deal with speculation problems and figuring out the nuts and bolts is a complex and often boring task. Some key steps should include increasing market transparency, monitoring speculative capital, and getting a collective agreement from major grain producers to pool a medium-sized international grain reserve that could be used to calm markets and lower prices when they greatly exceed those that markets fundamentals would dictate.[110]

Sixth, and perhaps most important from a long term perspective, there must be significant short, medium and long term investment increases in agricultural development and small farmers in developing countries. Most global development agencies have shifted their focus away from agriculture in recent decades, instead focusing on more popular and visible issues such as HIV/AIDS, malaria, or armed conflicts, but there are a number of reasons why they should begin to invest heavily again in agricultural programs. Moreover, there are many reasons why they should work to create a future global food market supplied to a large extent by the hundreds of millions of small farmers in developing countries. (It is useful here to quote a recent *Economist* article at length) :

-

"First, it would reduce poverty: three-quarters of those making do on $1 a day live in the countryside and depend on the health of smallholder farming. Next, it might help the environment: those smallholders manage a disproportionate share of the world's water and vegetation cover, so raising their productivity on existing land would be environmentally friendlier than cutting down the rainforest. And it should be efficient: in terms of returns on investment, it would be easier to boost grain yields in Africa from two tonnes per hectare to four than it would be to raise yields in Europe from eight tonnes to ten. The opportunities are greater and the law of diminishing returns has not set in."[111]

-

In addition, it could possibly reduce harmful urbanization by making rural life in poor countries more profitable and encouraging many slum dwellers to migrate back to the countryside, relieving deadly pressure on many growing "megacities" around the world.

Achieving this goal is much easier said than done, but there are concrete actions that should be taken in the short and long term. In the early stages, small farmers need increased access to seeds, fertilizers, and credit, and they should at least temporarily be guaranteed minimum prices for their products in order to incentivize increased production. In the past, these combined policies have been shown to vastly increase agricultural output in a variety of settings. While distribution of necessary inputs may need to be subsidized in some areas, the goal should be to also include the private sector from the outset and gradually shift to more sustainable market based programs.[112] A new $1.7 billion project by the UN's Food and Agriculture Organization to distribute seeds to farmers in developing countries is one example that should help greatly, but national governments and other branches of the UN will need to work together to maximize these and other funds.[113] In addition, banking and finance actors, especially micro-credit loans, will need to play an important role and should be adequately included into the organization of projects.

Further down the road other important long term investments need to be made. One hugely important sector is irrigation. As advancing climate change and growing populations stretch already strained water supplies even further, irrigation will have to both expand and become more effective, requiring billions of dollars in funding. In addition, more agricultural research and development in everything from seeds, to fertilizers, to storage mechanisms, to myriad other areas is desperately needed in order to achieve desired production increases, and will likely require sums reaching into the billions as well. This is an area where developed countries and aid organizations will need to play a large role because few developing states have the capabilities necessary for this type and scale of work. New productivity boosting innovations will also need to be employed as they arise, though affordability must always be considered because small farmers in poor countries will never be able to afford $500,000 combines or other expensive technologies. Many prominent figures have called for the use of genetically modified foods to play a large role in reshaping global agriculture, but it is still too early to determine whether they would have overall beneficial or harmful effects and they cannot be counted on alone. In the end it is necessary to keep in mind that because of the diversity of situations that different countries face the goal must not be to create a one-size-fits-all set of actions. Rather, local ownership of the process should and must be encouraged, though with a great deal of outside help.

As such, much of the investment in all of these projects will have to come from developing country governments themselves and they should plan to budget large levels of funds for agricultural projects that focus on the long term. Of course, aid organizations and developed states should provide large sums as well, as poor states lack the sufficient capital to achieve success alone and lower food prices are in the interests of all. Importantly, private sector finance should not be forgotten, as it can often exceed the levels and duration of available public funding. But increased agricultural development funds will not accomplish much if workers are sick or incapacitated, if roads, electricity, and communication access remain in deplorable conditions, or if farmers don't know the best techniques and have nowhere to store their crops once they have been harvested. Thus, large rural and urban investments will have to also be made in areas such as health, education communications, transportation, and infrastructure, in addition to those normally associated with agricultural and farming.[114]

Conclusion

Regardless of which options governments and international agencies take to counter the current crisis, for many people it may be too little too late. After decades of cheap food, high prices have ripped the seams of poverty and inequality ever wider across the globe, leaving hundreds of millions at risk of malnutrition or starvation and rolling back many of the recent gains made in poverty reduction. Even for the global middle classes who do not face mortal danger, the food crisis means a significant change in lifestyle that will push many back into poverty while hampering the efforts of those working to combat such outcomes. In both cause and effect the current crisis is global in every sense of the word, and it will require coordinated international effort and political will to solve. Moreover, this will not be a short-lived problem that simply fades away after a few months; it will take many years to fix global supply imbalances and thus any solutions need long term attention. Merely increasing food aid, while necessary, will not change the many systemic flaws that helped cause high prices, and without significant reform the current system will only further widen the gap between the global rich and poor, at both the local and national levels. If catastrophe is to be avoided much change will need to occur in the countries that house the world's poorest and most vulnerable people, from removing protectionist barriers to investing in poor farmers. Additionally, however, developed countries must take greater responsibility for the agricultural subsidies, market speculation, and misguided policies within their own borders that reduce supply, raise prices,

While the world watches with rapt attention as the global financial crisis unfolds it seems to have quickly forgotten the food crisis, despite the fact that the two are intertwined in complex ways.

and worsen the problem at the global level. The food crisis has already caused significant damage around the world and will assuredly create greater problems in the years to come, yet there is hope that it may be the impetus needed to create a more equitable and just global food system. However, to achieve this goal the myriad actors involved, from national governments, to the United Nations, to numerous other international organizations and major food producers, must come to agreement soon on how to move from mere ideas to implementation. If they don't we will be left with, in the words of one expert, "a lot of great intentions, but few results."[115] The world's poor certainly deserve better than that.

Addendum

Since September a lot has changed. The onset of the global financial crisis has dampened some aspects of the food crisis, such as high fuel and food prices, while worsening others, such as lower personal incomes, unemployment, and agricultural protectionism. Unfortunately for the poor this new crisis has only compounded their overall problems. As of December 2008 the prices of most major cereal crops had dropped 30-40 percent from their peak highs of last year and nearly all food prices have gone down significantly.[116] This has largely been due to a steep decrease in the price of fuel since the middle of 2008 – a barrel of oil that was selling for over $140 last May cost less than $40 in late February – that has subsequently reduced the costs of food production and transportation.[117] Despite this good news many problems remain. Prices for crops such as maize and wheat remain well above the levels of three or four years ago, meaning that they are still a significant burden for many of the world's poor.[118] For more developed countries, a recent report by the Institute for Agricultural and Trade Policy states that "The fall in commodity prices since July has not yet been transmitted to supermarket prices and it is unlikely that there will be a corresponding food retail price decrease in 2009."[119] Moreover, fuel prices will eventually rise again, bringing the costs of food up with them. As the head of the UN's Food and Agricultural Organization stated late last year, "The reduction in food prices should not be interpreted as the end of the food crisis."[120]

Additionally, the distribution of price decreases and their effect has been unequal. "In many countries the international price change is not quickly passed on to the domestic markets," says Joachim von Braun, noting that prices in most African countries are still well above traditional level.[121] This is often due to differing local conditions, such as natural time delays between purchase and delivery, the quality of supply routes and distribution programs, varying levels of import and export tariffs, and corruption. Cheaper prices have been great news for net food importing countries but have had a negative effect on net food exporters. In regions affected by conflict or political and economic instability – the very places that need cheap food the most – prices remain high: in Haiti the price of rice was double the global market value last fall and overall food prices in Afghanistan and Palestine were still 40 percent above 2007 levels in December.[122]

But food prices aren't the only important factor to consider. Capital investments in agriculture are vital for supply growth, increasing stockpiles and food security, yet in the face of the financial crisis these investments are at risk of setbacks. Small farmers are unlikely to get loans for investments due to reduced bank lending and many governments face immense macroeconomic and budgetary problems that will stymie efforts to improve agricultural growth.[123] Poor countries will undoubtedly fare worst, even though they are the ones who need to increase investment and productivity the most. In the meantime, many farmers rich and poor, big and small are cutting back on planting due to decreasing food prices and pessimistic economic outlooks for the future.[124] Such actions will only exacerbate supply shortages. Global food demand could drop somewhat as the financial crisis drives incomes down and unemployment up but population growth promises to keep upward pressure in place. As such, the supply-demand imbalance and supply distribution will continue to be significant problems. At the same time, speculation in food markets continues to run high, due in part to the fact that investors wary of other poor-performing sectors have pumped more money into commodities futures. Protectionist agricultural policies remain a popular tool for governments around the world, especially as the financial crisis has spread further and deeper, with China enacting a range of new exports tariffs on fertilizer in the fall. For their part, developed countries still show no hint of reducing their own inflated agricultural subsidies and the European Union has faced recent criticism for reinstating some dairy and poultry subsidies.[125]

Some substantive progress has been made at the international level in combating the food crisis but more must be done. Following the Rome Summit in May 2008 the World Bank's Global Food Crisis Response Program (GFRP) "put half a billion dollars on the ground...with about 60 percent of the amount in the form of seeds and fertilizer, including 250,000 tons of fertilizer and 1,500 tons of seed for 2.4 million small farms in the Kyrgyz Republic, Tajikistan, Somalia, Niger, Ethiopia and Togo at crucial times of the agriculture calendar."[126] Other funds have been used to support the budgets of countries who have removed food taxes and tariffs and to extend safety net programs for children and pregnant women.[127] Despite these actions only twenty percent of billions of dollars committed in Rome have been dispersed.[128] In January another high-level conference on the food crisis was held in Madrid, where over one hundred countries promised further monetary aid and commitment to promoting small farmers and agricultural productivity in developing countries. However, some participants noted that "'no substantial discussion took place' and there was 'no real confrontation of the problem' of the current model of agricultural production."[129] Thus, solutions to the problems of high food prices, unequal food distribution, protectionism, and long-term supply, demand and productivity issues remain elusive.

We are not out of the woods yet. While the world watches with rapt attention as the global financial crisis unfolds it seems to have quickly forgotten the food crisis, despite the fact that the two are intertwined in complex ways. Commodity prices have dropped significantly since last year's highs, thanks in no small part to a global financial meltdown, but this new crisis has created gravely serious troubles that continue to threaten the availability and price of food around the globe. From the Ukraine to the United States, Chile to China economic slowdowns have pushed tens of millions out of work and reduced incomes, in the majority of cases outweighing any benefit offered by cheaper food. Investments in agriculture are being cut, despite the long-term negative effects this will cause, and protectionism will continue to disrupt food distribution and keep prices unnecessarily high. Many commitments and immense sums have been promised to deal with the global food crisis, but few governments seem willing to disperse these funds as global financial problems grow ever larger. While the current financial crisis must be addressed effectively, it would be a disastrous mistake to forget about the food crisis. At this point significant dilemmas will remain even after the major problems have been addressed; for example the effects of poor nutrition, especially among children, will continue to reverberate long after the crisis has ended.[130] Unfortunately, my final words written ten months ago still apply today: governmental and international actors need to delineate responsibilities and begin acting on their promises. Intentions are certainly great, but results thus far have been anything but.

/ END

Notes
1 "Haitian prime minister ousted over high food prices."
2 Ibid
3 "Cheap no more"
4 "Cheap no more."
5 Conway, Chapter 4.
6 Streitfeld, David. "In Price and Supply."
7 Ibid.
8 "Cheap no more."
9 Faiola, Anthony. "The New Economics of Hunger."
10 von Braun, Joachim. "Rising Food Prices: What Should Be Done?"
11 "The new face of hunger."
12 "World Food Situation."
13 Streitfeld, David. "In Price and Supply."
14 Black, Jane. "Clipping, Scrimping, Saving."
15 von Braun, Joachim. "Rising Food Prices: What Should Be Done?"
16 Teslik, Lee Hudson. "Backgrounder: Food Prices."
17 "The new face of hunger."
18 Ibid
19 Wilkinson, Tracy. "World Food Programme issues 'emergency appeal' for funds."
20 "Food Price Crisis Imperils 100 Million in Poor Countries, Zoellick Says."
21 Walt, Vivienne. "The World's Growing Food-Price Crisis."
22 "WFP: Cash roll-out to help hunger spots."
23 Black, Jane. "Clipping, Scrimping, Saving."
24 Anti-government rioting spreads in Cameroon."
25 "Egyptian boy dies from wounds sustained in Mahalla riots."
26 "The cost of food: Facts and figures."
27 Bradsher, Keith. "Vietnam and India move to limit rice exports."
28 von Braun, Joachim. "Rising Food Prices: What Should Be Done?"
29 von Braun, Joachim, et al. "High Food Prices: The Who, What, and How of Proposed Policy Actions."
30 "UN and World Bank say to tackle crisis."
31 "Food Price Crisis Imperils 100 Million in Poor Countries, Zoellick Says."
32 "UN and World Bank say to tackle crisis."
33 "The world food summit."
34 von Braun, Joachim. "Food Summit: Some Progress But More Needs to be Done."
35 Tate, Deborah. "US Senate Panel Considers Response to Global Food Crisis."
36 "Bush proposes $700 million for world food crisis."
37 Jagger, Suzy and David Charter. "Food crisis: rationing introduced in bid to protect rice supplies."
38 Mufson, Steven. "Siphoning Off Corn to Fuel Our Cars."
39 Ibida
40 "Making a killing from hunger." and Kesmodel, David and Lauren Etter and Aaron O. Patrick. "Grain companies' profits soar as global food crisis mounts."
41 Pfaff, William. "Speculators and soaring food prices."
42 "Cheap no more."
43 Streitfeld, David. "In Price and Supply."
44 "Cheap no more."
45 Teslik, Lee Hudson. "Backgrounder: Food Prices."
46 Streitfeld, David. "A Global Need for Grain the Farmers Can't Fill."
47 "The cost of food: Facts and figures."
48 Streitfeld, David. "A Global Need for Grain That Farmers Can't Fill."
49 Mouawad, Jad. "Oil Price Rise Fails to Open Tap." and "Oil Rises as Consumer Confidence Gains."
50 Bradsher, Keith and Andrew Martin. "Shortages threaten farmers' key tool: fertilizer."
51 Mufson, Steven. "Siphoning Off Corn to Fuel Our Cars."
52 Ibid.
53 Ibid.
54 von Braun, Joachim. "Biofuels, International Food Prices, and the Poor."
55 Faiola, Anthony. "The New Economics of Hunger."
56 Gary, Bill. "Global Grain Shortage of Historic Proportions Ahead."
57 Faiola, Anthony. "The New Economics of Hunger."
58 Young, John E. "Speculation and World Food Markets."
59 Ibid
60 Pfaff, William. "Speculators and soaring food prices."
61 Ibid
62 Young, John E. "Speculation and World Food Markets."
63 Faiola, Anthony. "The New Economics of Hunger."
64 Ibid
65 Minot, Nicholas. "The Food Crisis and its Implications for Agricultural Development."
66 "Cheap no more."
67 von Braun, Joachim. "Rising Food Prices: What Should Be Done?"
68 "Cheap no more."
69 "The new face of hunger."
70 Rice, p13.
71 Streitfeld, David. "A Global Need for Grain That Farmers Can't Fill."
72 Bradsher, Keith and Andrew Martin. "Shortages threaten farmers' key tool: fertilizer."
73 Ibid
74 Eggen, Dan. "U.S. Scrambles to Address International Food Crisis."
75 Mufson, Steven. "Siphoning Off Corn to Fuel Our Cars."
76 "Higher food prices here to stay: World Bank."
77 "The cost of food: Facts and figures."
78 "Cheap no more."
79 Ibid
80 Ibid
81 Ibid
82 von Braun, Joachim, et al. "High Food Prices: The Who, What, and How of Proposed Policy Actions."
83 Ibid
84 "The new face of hunger."
85 Faiola, Anthony. "Where Every Meal Is a Sacrifice." and "Mauritania at a glance."
86 Bradsher, Keith and Andrew Martin. "Shortages threaten farmers' key tool: fertilizer."
87 Food prices and protest.
88 "World Publics Welcome Global Trade – But Not Immigration."
89 Pfaff, William. "Speculators and soaring food prices."
90 Faiola, Anthony. "The New Economics of Hunger."
91 Faiola, Anthony. "Where Every Meal Is a Sacrifice."
92 Ibid
93 "How to Feed the World." and "The world food summit."
94 von Braun, Joachim, et al. "High Food Prices: The Who, What, and How of Proposed Policy Actions."
95 "How Will Rising Food Prices Impact the World?"
96 Searchinger, Timothy et al. "Use of U.S. Croplands for Biofuels Increases Greenhouse Gases Through Emissions from Land Use Change."
97 von Braun, Joachim, et al. "High Food Prices: The Who, What, and How of Proposed Policy Actions."
98 "UN and World Bank say to tackle crisis."
99 "Cheap no more."
100 Ibid
101 von Braun, Joachim, et al. "High Food Prices: The Who, What, and How of Proposed Policy Actions."
102 "Cheap no more."
103 "The politics of rising food prices in Africa."
104 von Braun, Joachim. "Rising Food Prices: What Should Be Done?"
105 Faiola, Anthony. "The New Economics of Hunger."
106 Faiola, Anthony. "Where Every Meal Is a Sacrifice."
107 Hamm, Steve. "Solutions from a hunger crisis."
108 Collier, p160 and Ibid.

[10 9] Henriques, Diana B. "Price Volatility Adds to Worry on U.S. Farms."

[110] von Braun, Joachim, et al. "High Food Prices: The Who, What, and How of Proposed Policy Actions."

[111] "The new face of hunger."

[112] von Braun, Joachim, et al. "High Food Prices: The Who, What, and How of Proposed Policy Actions."

[113] "UN to set up task force on food crisis."

[114] von Braun, Joachim. "Rising Food Prices: What Should Be Done?"

[115] von Braun, Joachim. "Food Summit: Some Progress But More Needs to be Done."

[116] von Braun, Joachim. "Food and Financial Crises: Implications for Agriculture and the Poor."

[117] "Oil prices end week on the down side."

[118] von Braun, Joachim. "Food and Financial Crises: Implications for Agriculture and the Poor."

[119] Suppan, Steve. "Betting Against Food Security: Futures Market Speculation."

[120] Borrell, Brendan. "Back from the Brink: Global Financial Meltdown Relieves Food Crisis."

[121] Biello, David. "Has the Food Crisis Abated?"

[122] Ibid.

[123] von Braun, Joachim. "Food and Financial Crises: Implications for Agriculture and the Poor."

[124] Cha, Ariana Eunjung and Stephanie McCrummen. "Financial Meltdown Worsens Food Crisis."

[125] Ibid, and "Madrid Agriculture Meeting Tackles 'Forgotten' Food Crisis."

[126] "Food Security Focus of Madrid Meeting."

[127] Ibid.

[128] "Madrid Agriculture Meeting Tackles 'Forgotten' Food Crisis."

[129] Ibid.

[130] von Braun, Joachim. "Food and Financial Crises: Implications for Agriculture and the Poor."


Works Referenced

"Agflation: The real costs of rising food prices." Reuters.com. 29 Apr 2008. <http://www.reuters.com/news/globalcoverage/agflation>.

"Anti-government rioting spreads in Cameroon." International Herald Tribune.com. 27 Feb 2008. 27 Apr 2008. <http://www.iht.com/articles/2008/02/27/africa/27cameroon.php>.

Arends, Brent. "Load Up the Pantry." Wall Street Journal.com. 21 Apr 2008. 28 Apr 2008. <http://online.wsj.com/article/SB120881517227532621.html>.

Biello, David. "Has the Food Crisis Abated?" Scientific American.com. 15 Dec 2008. 25 Feb 2009. <http://www.sciam.com/article.cfm?id=has-the-food-crisis-abated>.

Black, Jane. "Clipping, Scrimping, Saving." Washington Post.com. 1 May 2008. 1 May 2008. <http://www.washingtonpost.com/wp-dyn/content/article/2008/04/30/AR20 08043003435.html>.

Borrell, Brendan. "Back from the Brink: Global Financial Meltdown Relieves Food Crisis." Scientific American.com. 9 Dec 2008. 25 Feb 2009. <http://www.sciam.com/article.cfm?id=from-finances-to-food-crisis>.

Bradsher, Keith. "Vietnam and India move to limit rice exports." International Herald Tribune.com. 29 Mar 2008. 31 Apr 2008. <http://www.iht.com/articles/2008/03/28/business/rice.php>.

Bradsher, Keith and Andrew Martin. "Shortages threaten farmers' key tool: fertilizer." International Herald Tribune.com. 30 Apr 2008. 1 May 2008. <http://www.iht.com /articles/2008/04/30/business/30fertilizer.php>.

"Bush proposes $700 million for world food crisis." Reuters.com. 1 May 2008. 1 May 2008. <http://www.reuters.com/article/GCA-Agflation/idUSN0154468120080501>.

Cha, Ariana Eunjung and Stephanie McCrummen. "Financial Meltdown Worsens Food Crisis." Washington Post.com. 26 Oct 2008. 27 Feb 2009. <http://www.washingtonpost.com/wp-dyn/content/article/2008/10/25AR200810250

2293.html>.

"Cheap no more." Economist.com. 6 Dec 2007. 26 Apr 2008. <http://www.economist.com/ displaystory.cfm?story_id=10250420>.

Collier, Paul. The Bottom Billion: Why the Poorest Countries Are Failing and What Can Be Done About It. Oxford: Oxford University Press, 2007.

Conway, Gordon. The Doubly Green Revolution. Ithaca: Cornell University Press, 1998.

Eggen, Dan. "U.S. Scrambles to Address International Food Crisis." Washington Post.com. 26 Apr 2008. 28 Apr 2008. <http://www.washingtonpost.com/wp-dyn/content/article/2008/04/25/AR2008042503278.html?hpid=topnews>.

"Egyptian boy dies from wounds sustained in Mahalla riots." International Herald Tribune.com. 8 Apr 2008. 26 Apr 2008. <http://www.iht.com/articles/ap/2008/04/08/africa/ME-GEN-Egypt-Protest-Death.php>.

Faiola, Anthony. "Where Every Meal Is a Sacrifice." Washington Post.com. 28 Apr 2008. 28 Apr 2008. <http://www.washingtonpost.com/wp-dyn/content/story/2008/04/ 27/ST2008042702198.html>.

Faiola, Anthony. "The New Economics of Hunger." Washington Post.com. 27 Apr 2008. 27 Apr 2008. <http://www.washingtonpost.com/wp-dyn/content/story/2008/04/26/ST2008 042602333.html>.

"Food for thought." Economist.com. 27 Mar 2008. 3 May 2008. < http://www.economist.com/ world/international/displaystory.cfm?story_id=10925518>.

"Food Price Crisis Imperils 100 Million in Poor Countries, Zoellick Says." World Bank.org. 14 Apr 2008. 31 Apr 2008. <http://web.worldbank.org/WBSITE/EXTERNAL/NEWS/0,,contentMDK:21729143~pagePK:64257043~piPK:437 376~theSitePK:4607,00.html>.

"Food prices and protest." Economist.com. 8 May 2008. 28 Aug 2008. <http://www.economist.com/world/international/displaystory.cfm?story_id=1133 2931>.

"Food prices could spark protectionism in Africa: IMF." Reuters.com. 17 Apr 2008. 4 May 2008. <http://www.reuters.com/article/idUSL1786734820080417>.

"Food prices rising across the world." CNN.com. 25 Mar 2008. 29 Apr 2008. <http://www.cnn. com/2008/WORLD/americas/03/24/food.ap/>.

"Food Security Focus of Madrid Meeting." World Bank.org. 23 Jan 2009. 25 Feb 2009. <http://web.worldbank.org/WBSITE/EXTERNAL/NEWS/0,,contentMDK:22043218~pagePK:64257043~piPK:437376~theSitePK:4607,00.html>.

Fuller, Thomas. "5 Asian Nations Are Weighing a Rice Cartel." New York Times.com. 1 May 2008. 1 May 2008. <http://www.nytimes.com/2008/05/01/business/worldbusiness/01 cartel.html?ex=1210305600&en=53ba1ab928d80c a1&ei=5070&emc=eta1>.

Fuller, Thomas. "Soaring Food Prices Imperil Meals for Poor in Cambodia." New York Times.com. 30 Apr 2008. 1 May 2008. <http://www.nytimes.com/2008/04/30/ world/asia/30cambodia.html?_r=1&ref=world&oref=slogin>.

Gary, Bill. "Global Grain Shortage of Historic Proportions Ahead." Commodity Information Systems, Inc. 1 May 2008. <http://www.mmdnewswire.com/global-grain-shortage-of-historic-proportions-ahead-1257-2.html>.

"Haitian prime minister ousted over high food prices." CNN.com. 21 Apr 2008. 28 Apr 2008. <http://www.cnn.com/2008/WORLD/americas/04/12/haiti.ap/>.

Hamm, Steve. "Solutions from a hunger crisis." Businessweek.com. 1 May 2008. 1 May 2008. <http://www.businessweek.com/magazine/content/08_19/b4083026413508.htm>.

Henriques, Diana B. "Price Volatility Adds to Worry on U.S. Farms." New York Times.com. 22 Apr 2008. 2 May 2008. <http://www.nytimes.com/2008/04/22/business/22 commodity.html?ref=business>.

"Higher food prices here to stay: World Bank." Reuters.com. 9 Apr 2008. 30 Apr 2008. <http://www.reuters.com/article/topNews/idUSWAT00929720 080409?feedType=RSS&feedName=topNews>.

"How Will Rising Food Prices Impact the World?" Newsweek and Washington Post. 30 Apr 2008. <http://newsweek.washingtonpost.com/postglobal/2008/04/how_will_rising_food_prices_im/>.

"How to Feed the World." Newsweek.com. 19 May 2008. 27 Aug 2008. <http://www.newsweek.com/id/136360/page/1>.

Jagger, Suzy and David Charter. "Food crisis: rationing introduced in bid to

DISCOURSE

THE FORGOTTEN CRISIS
HOW HIGH FOOD PRICES HAVE
IMPOVERISHED MILLIONS AND
THREATENED GOVERNMENTS

AUSTIN BLAIR SIADAK

39

30 OF 30

protect rice supplies." TimesOnline. 24 Apr 2008. 29 Apr 2008. <http://business. timesonline.co.uk /tol/business/industry_sectors/retailing/article3803738.ece>.

Kesmodel, David and Lauren Etter and Aaron O. Patrick. "Grain companies' profits soar as global food crisis mounts." TucsonCitizen.com. 30 Apr 2008. 1 May 2008. <http://www.tucsoncitizen.com/daily/breakingnews/83971.php>.

Kingsbury, Kathleen. "After the Oil Crisis, a Food Crisis?" Time.com. 16 Nov 2007. 28 Apr 2008. <http://www.time.com/time/business/article/0,8599,1684 910,00.html?iid=sphere-inline-sidebar>.

"Madrid Agriculture Meeting Tackles 'Forgotten' Food Crisis." International Centre for Trade and Sustainable Development. 6 Feb 2009. 27 Feb 2009. <http:// ictsd.net/i/news/biores/40099/>.

"Making a killing from hunger." Grain.org. 1 May 2008. <http://www.grain. org/articles/?id=39>

"Mauritania at a glance." World Bank. 28 Sep 2007. 28 Aug 2008. <http:// devdata.worldbank. org/AAG/mrt_aag.pdf>.

Minot, Nicholas. "The Food Crisis and its Implications for Agricultural Development." House Committee on Agriculture. Testimony presented to Subcommittee on Specialty Crops, Rural Development, and Foreign Agriculture. 16 Jul 2008. 27 Aug 2008. <http://agriculture.house.gov/testimony/110/h80716/ Minot.pdf>.

Morgan, Dan. "Emptying the Breadbasket." Washington Post.com. 29 Apr 2008. 29 Apr 2008. <http://www.washingtonpost.com/wp-dyn/content/article/ 2008/04/28/AR200804 2802509.html?sub=new>.

Mouawad, Jad. "Oil Price Rise Fails to Open Tap." New York Times.com. 29 Apr 2008. 9 May 2008. <http://www.nytimes.com/2008/04/29/business/world business/29oil.html?ref=todayspaper>.

Mufson, Steven. "Siphoning Off Corn to Fuel Our Cars." Washington Post. com. 30 Apr 2008. 30 Apr 2008. <http://www.washingtonpost.com/wp-dyn/ content/article/2008/04/29/AR2008042903092.html>.

"Oil prices end the week on the down side." MSNBC.com. 27 Feb 2009. 27 Feb 2009. <http://www.msnbc.msn.com/id/12400801/>.

"Oil Rises as Consumer Confidence Gains." New York Times.com. 26 Aug 2008. 27 Aug 2008. <http://www.nytimes.com/2008/08/27/business/27stox. html?scp=3&sq=oil%20price&st=cse>.

Pfaff, William. "Speculators and soaring food prices." International Herald Tribune.com. 16 Apr 2008. 30 Apr 2008. <http://www.iht.com/articles/2008/04/ 16/opinion/edpfaff.php>.

Rice, Susan. "The Tangled Web: The Poverty-Insecurity Nexus." Too Poor for Peace?: Global Poverty, Conflict, and Security in the 21st Century. Eds. Lael Brainard and Derek Chollet. Washington: Brookings Institution Press: 2007.

Searchinger, Timothy et al. "Use of U.S. Croplands for Biofuels Increases Greenhouse Gases Through Emissions from Land Use Change." Sciencemag. org. 7 Feb 2008. 3 May 2008. <http://www.sciencemag.org/cgi/content/abstra ct/1151861v1?maxtoshow=&HITS=10&hits=10&RESULTFORMAT=&fulltext =Searchinger+&searchid=1&FIRSTINDEX=0&resourcetype=HWCIT>.

Streitfeld, David. "A Global Need for Grain That Farmers Can't Fill." New York Times.com. 9 Mar 2008. 26 Apr 2008. <http://www.nytimes.com/2008/03 /09/business/worldbusi ness/09crop.html?scp=3&sq=streitfeld&st=nyt>.

Streitfeld, David. "In Price and Supply, Wheat is the Unstable Staple." New York Times.com. 13 Feb 2008. 30 Apr 2008. <http://www.nytimes.com/2008/03/ 09/business/world business/09crop.html?_r=1&scp=3&sq=streitfeld&st=nyt &oref=login>.

Suppan, Steve. "Betting Against Food Security: Futures Market Speculation." Institute for Agriculture and Trade Policy. Jan 2009. 26 Feb 2009. <http://www. iatp.org/iatp/publications.cfm?refid=105065>.

Tate, Deborah. "US Senate Panel Considers Response to Global Food Crisis." Voice of America.com. 14 May 2008. 26 Aug 2008. <http://www.voanews.com/ english/archive /2008-05/2008-05-14-voa62.cfm>.

Teslik, Lee Hudson. "Backgrounder: Food Prices." New York Times.com. 30 Jun 2008. 26 Aug 2008. <http://www.nytimes.com/cfr/world/slot1_20080 630.html?ref=world>.

"The cost of food: Facts and figures." BBC.com. 8 Apr 2008. 26 Apr 2008. <http://news.bbc. co.uk/2/hi/in_depth/7284196.stm>.

"The Global Grain Bubble." CSMonitor.com. 18 Jan 2008. 2 May 2008. <http:// www.csmonitor .com/2008/0118/p08s01-comv.html>.

"The new face of hunger." Economist.com. 17 Apr 2008. 29 Apr 2008. <http:// www.economist.com/world/international/displaystory.cfm?story_id=11049284>.

"The politics of fast rising food prices in Africa." The Nigerian Tribune. 14 May 2008. 27 Aug 2008. <http://www.tribune.com.ng/14052008/biznes.html>.

"The world food summit." Economist.com. 5 Jun 2008. 26 Aug 2008. <http:// www.economist.com/world/international/displaystory.cfm?story_id=11502285>.

"Too Many Babies?" Economist.com. 24 Apr 2008. 28 Apr 2008. <http:// www.economist.com /world/asia/displaystory.cfm?story_id=11090635>.

"U.N. officials blame market speculation for recent food price jump." International Herald Tribune.com. 28 Apr 2008. 30 Apr 2008. <http://www. iht.com/articles/ap/2008/ 04/28/news/UN-Food-Crisis.php>.

"UN and World Bank say to tackle crisis." Reuters.com. 29 Apr 2008. 31 Apr 2008. <http://www.reuters.com/article/topNews/idUSL2971907120080429?p ageNumber=1&virtualBrandChannel=0>.

"UN to set up task force on food crisis." International Herald Tribune.com. 29 Apr 2008. 30 Apr 2008. <http://www.iht.com/articles/2008/04/29/europe/ 30food.php>.

von Brain, Joachim. "Biofuels, International Food Prices, and the Poor." International Food Policy Research Institute.org. 12 June 2008. 27 Aug 2008. <http://www.ifpri.org/pubs/testimony/vonbraun20080612.asp

von Braun, Joachim. "Food and Financial Crises: Implications for Agriculture and the Poor." International Food Policy Research Institute.org. Dec 2008. 26 Feb 2009. <http://www.ifpri.org/pubs/fpr/pr20all.asp>.

von Braun, Joachim. "Food Summit: Some Progress But More Needs to be Done." International Food Policy Research Institute.org. 6 June 2008. 26 Aug 2008. <http://www.ifpri.org /pressrel/2008/20080606.asp>.

von Braun, Joachim, et al. "High Food Prices: The What, Who, and How of Proposed Policy Actions." International Food Policy Research Institute.org. May 2008. 26 Aug 2008. <http://www.ifpri.org/PUBS/ib/FoodPricesPolicyAction.pdf>.

von Braun, Joachim. "Rising Food Prices: What Should be Done?" International Food Policy Research Institute.org. April 2008. 28 Apr 2008. <http:// www.ifpri.org/pubs/bp/bp001. asp>.

Walt, Vivienne. "The World's Growing Food-Price Crisis." Time.com. 27 Feb 2008. 28 Apr 2008. <http://www.time.com/time/world/article/0,8599,1717572, 00.html>.

Wallace, Bruce. "Price of rice takes toll in Asian slums." Boston.com. 27 Apr 2008. 27 Apr 2008. <http://www.boston.com/news/world/asia/articles/2008/04/ 27/price_of_ rice_takes_toll_in_asian_slums/?p1=email_to_a_friend>.

Wilkinson, Tracy. "World Food Programme issues 'emergency appeal' for funds." Los Angeles Times.com. 25 Mar 2008. 30 Apr 2008. <http://www.latimes. com/news/nationworld/ world/la-fg-food25mar25,1,7719765.story?track=rss>.

"WFP: Cash roll-out to help hunger spots." World Food Programme.org. 12 Aug 2008. 26 Aug 2008. <http://www.wfp.org/english/?Key=2899&Modul eID=137>.

"WFP says high food prices a silent tsunami, affecting every continent." World Food Programme.org. 22 Apr 2008. 27 Apr 2008. <http://www.wfp.org/ english/?ModuleID= 137&Key=2820>.

"What Global Food Prices Mean for WFP." World Food Programme.org. 20 Mar 2008. 25 Apr 2008. <http://www.wfp.org/english/?ModuleID=137&K ey=2797>.

"Why the era of cheap food is over." CSMonitor.com. 31 Dec 2007. 30 Apr 2008. <http://www. csmonitor.com/2007/1231/p13s01-wogi.html>.

"World Food Situation: Food Prices Indices." Food and Agriculture Organization of the United Nations. April 2008. 29 Apr 2008. <http://www.fao. org/worldfoodsituation/ FoodPricesIndex>.

"World Publics Welcome Global Trade – But Not Immigration." Pew Global Attitudes Project. 4 Oct 2007. 3 May 2008. <http://pewresearch.org/pubs/607/ global-trade-immigration>.

Young, John E. "Speculation and World Food Markets." International Food Policy Research Institute.com. IFPRI Forum, July 2008. 27 Aug 2008. <http://www.ifpri.org/PUBS/ newsletters/IFPRIForum/if22.pdf>.

# DO N
# THE S
# DEVE

AN INSTITUTE
FOR GLOBAL LEADERSHIP
DR. JEAN MAYER GLOBAL
CITIZENSHIP LECTURE

ASHRAF GHANI

O HARM?
CURITY
OPMENT
COMPLEX

Ashraf Ghani played a central role in the design and implementation of the post-Taliban settlement in Afghanistan, serving as United Nations adviser to the Bonn process and as Finance Minister during Afghanistan's Transitional Administration. He designed the national development strategy and carried out a series of successful reforms that won him Emerging Markets' Best Finance Minister Asia award in 2003. He served on the faculty of Berkeley, Johns Hopkins, and Kabul University and spent a decade at the World Bank, leading work on numerous country strategies. He has been nominated for the job of Secretary General of the United Nations and considered for the job of President of the World Bank. He is the founder and chair of the Institute for State Effectiveness. He is also the coauthor of *Fixing Failed States: A Framework for Rebuilding a Fractured World*. In February 2008, he received the Dr. Jean Mayer Global Citizenship Award from the Institute for Global Leadership at Tufts University. This is the address he gave then, with excerpts from the question and answer session.

What defines a life? A life comes out of a commitment. Mine was defined by my grandmother. She was an educated woman, a rare breed. My family has been dispossessed for seven generations, every generation. We lost everything. Every generation. Wrong side of a foreign invasion, wrong side of a civil war. But one of the outcomes was that at one point, all my family went into exile. As a result, my grandmother was educated. And when she came back, at the time when they did not believe in education, she insisted that we acquire education. In second grade, I refused to go to school one day, and it's the only time that she's touched me physically, saying that that was non-negotiable. Afterward, when she was complaining that I was spending too much time on my Master's or my PhD, I would turn back and say, "Grandmother, you said that was non-negotiable."

The quest for learning has to come from a problem, and the problem that I've dealt with has been the question of how do you create a level playing field for people of diverse backgrounds in order to be able to join in a common quest for moving forward.

It is both an honor and privilege to be here with you to receive the Mayer Award, particularly because Jean Mayer exemplified what I'd like to call the best of pragmatic idealism. He deeply believed in equity and commitment to the poor and saw public policy as the critical instrument necessary to create a level playing field for the excluded and underprivileged.

In preparation for this talk, I was reviewing Mayer's work and was struck in particular by the Lowell Lecture he made on 15 May 1989, and I would recommend that you all read it. He focused that day on food policy, arguing that, and I quote, "Science by itself does not constitute nutrition unless and until a program of action is incorporated as part of the discipline." Mayer pointed out that greater knowledge brings greater responsibility, and only if you involve the middle class in a reform effort involving the poor will you meet with success.

He also formulated the groundbreaking doctrine of nutrition rights, inspired by the concept of civil rights, which spearheaded the formulation of food programs in the U.S., targeting children in particular. Finally, he criticized the inefficiency of international aid, arguing that the generosity of spirit that produced the Marshall Plan had given way to ineffective and counterproductive aid practices. These insights are as relevant today as they were in May 1989.

I thought a focus on three issues that are of critical importance to us – hunger, development security, and the environment – would provide an interesting basis for understanding Mayer's impressions, exploring how the international aid syndrome is so ineffective, and how we can best improve the way things work.

The FAO (Food and Agricultural Organization) now estimates that about 850 million people around the world are currently undernourished. Isn't this the shame of our times? With so much plenty, still 850 million people undernourished. That's the dimension of the problem that Mayer identified that is clearly very much with us. The number of food and humanitarian emergencies has doubled, from 15 per year in 1980 to more than 30 since 2000, as a result of poverty, conflict, and natural disasters.

US food aid averages around $2 billion a year in annual and supplemental funding by Congress, and the estimated number of beneficiaries has been around 70 million people. Two billion dollars but only 70 millions mouths fed because the cost of management and logistics constitutes 65 percent of US food aid. Sixty-five percent of the food aid is spent on management and logistics. The current rules and regulations that require support for the American private sector prevent efficiency. For example, cargo preference laws require 75 percent of food aid to be shipped on US flag carriers, which are more costly than many other national carriers. This inefficiency is counterproductive and avoidable, as Mayer well understood.

If we want to act pro-poor, we need to change the rules of the game that the powerful set for creating the instruments for working with the poor. Changing the playing field on poverty begins with the top. In Afghanistan, the unintended impact of food aid on the ground was the exacerbation of poverty and, at times, a shift to criminality.

Representing the Afghan government in 2002, I argued strongly with food providers that markets were efficient in Afghanistan and that given the seasonality of production, because we have a six-month period over which wheat matures, one needed to support the market to signal to farmers that their products were valuable. This required the use of modern technology to estimate domestic production and the careful use of food assistance at the right time and the right place. However, instead of a carefully calibrated strategy, the World Food Program (WFP) released large quantities of food indiscriminately. For the first time in our history, Afghan farmers found it unprofitable to harvest wheat because the cost of food at the market was lower than the cost of production.

In the next two years we also saw a massive shift in the production of opium. While there is not a direct cause and effect relationship between the two, it is indisputable that there was a lack of alignment between the type of support that would reinforce food production by the poor and the food damping approach by the international community.

The targeting of food distribution has been a huge problem. In Afghanistan, relying on cash for work would have reinforced local market relationships and investment in agriculture productivity, and would have been more successful. But the aid system acts against the rational interests of the poor. The core issue is that we need to deal with the causes of hunger, not the symptoms. The poor do not need charity. They need effective interventions. Charity makes us feel good, but it makes the poor feel awful. And we need to change this fundamental relationship.

Dealing with the causes means three central tasks. Firstly, renewing a commitment to pro-poor agricultural policies that reduce poverty. The nature of public intervention needs to be different, with an emphasis on building effective markets and ensuring that the United States and Europe reform agricultural subsidies. The amount that the United States and Europe provide in agricultural subsidies is the greatest disincentive to food production in the rest of the world. When 75 percent of US charity is spent on administrative costs, it is privileging a sector of American business, not the poor.

Secondly, we need to apply modern agricultural techniques where they are needed. The science of agriculture is very advanced, but it has yet to find its Jean Mayer, that is to find its champions that can turn the science into a basis for an agenda for action in developing countries. Land grant colleges, created and funded as part of pro-poor public policy in the United States, have played a vital role in the development of agriculture in the United

The FAO (Food and Agricultural Organization) now estimates that about 850 million people around the world are currently undernourished. Isn't this the shame of our times?

States. These colleges and the knowledge that they embody need to be linked to a global agenda for agriculture reform and to partner with institutions in developing countries.

And thirdly, social policies to reach the ultra poor need to be thought through. Current social policies, where it takes five dollars to deliver one dollar, are not the way to proceed. And we need to think about instruments again in fundamentally new ways.

Food aid is one aspect of aid. The aid discourse has become focused on poverty, empowerment, inclusion, gender – all the right words. But there is a disconnect between that discourse and the instruments for the realization of those goals.

Let me take just a couple of examples. American aid has been captured by a development security complex that is strongly entrenched to a powerful set of interest groups, such as shipping and agricultural lobbying, NGOs, and Congress.

The Government Accountability Office (GAO) explains that the Department of Defense continues to lack the capability to provide information on the totality of contractor support to deploy forces. In the Balkans in 2002, the Department of Defense was unaware of the number of contractors operating, the tasks they were contracted to do, and the government's obligations to these contractors under their contracts. The reports indicated that the situation in southwest Asia and Kosovo was similar in 2003. Their record of delivery of aid is damning in Iraq. The GAO has recently released the report entitled "Stabilizing and Rebuilding Iraq: Conditions in Iraq are Conducive to Fraud, Waste, and Abuse." That's the title. The report details a heavy reliance on contractors, with the Department of Defense entering into contract arrangements on reconstruction efforts that posed additional risks to the government, with officials again unable to determine how many contractors were deployed and therefore the costs of those contracts. As of March 2004, about $1.8 billion had been obligated to reconstruction contract actions without the Department of Defense and the contractors reaching agreement on the final scope and the cost of the work. An additional $18 billion was handled in similar ways. The net result is a lack of strategic focus. The report argues, "that US planning efforts have been plagued by unclear

goals and objectives, changing priorities, inadequate risk assessment, and uncertain costs."

In Afghanistan, as the person in charge of development planning between 2002-2004, my priority was to connect the Northern provinces with the South. I obtained financing from the World Bank which, through its procurement process, sent an American firm to carry out the construction of the Kabul-Kunduz road. I then focused on support for the Kabul-Kandahar road in the South. With support from USAID, the same American contracting firm was chosen. This firm promptly shifted all its attention to the southern road, because that was the priority of the US President, and entirely neglected the northern road. This caused immense political difficulties in terms of the perception of equity among northerners. I had promised change and had obtained the money to deliver on that change.

This had an incalculable effect on the government's legitimacy, given that building trust in post-conflict environments is an essential task. Most USAID contracts are assigned to six firms, all from around the beltway, which in turn subcontract out to as many as six layers. The end result is that as little as ten cents of every American dollar is actually spent inside the country it is purporting to help.

The Government of Afghanistan had a clear development strategy by April 2002, to which the rest of the international community was increasingly buying in. We convened the first Afghanistan development forum after the devastation of the Taliban, believe it or not, in April of 2002. In Kabul, chaired by us, and unlike any other meetings, I wrote all of the speeches of the foreigners. Because when the World Bank came to offer to write my speech I said, "This is what I used to do for others, why do I need you?" Then we developed a strategy to secure Afghanistan's future and that was presented to the international community in April of 2004, in Berlin, and received endorsements from over 60 finance and foreign ministers.

However, by the end of 2004, USAID, as again pointed out by the GAO, had not only failed to develop a strategy for Afghanistan for its own expenditures, but it actively refused to buy into ours, creating parallel institutions and organizations. As a result, the public has become disenchanted with the slow pace of development and the lack of transparency and accountability of American-led development efforts. The developed world has developed a habit of lecturing to the underdeveloped world on its lack of accountability and transparency. I'd like to submit the evidence to you as to who lacks transparency and accountability.

The pattern that emerges from these examples is that outsourcing of government functions in the United States has reached a point where accountability has evaporated. Noble intentions are frustrated by the reality of practice. Time and again, audit reports point to the fact that food aid and foreign aid supervision are extremely limited, but little change is put into practice. Audit reports are fantastic documents if you really want to know what's happening. They require mastery of language as arcane as any, but once one has mastered it, they provide the dye that provides the food diagnostic. It is not enough just to focus on increasing aid.

There's a very well meaning lobby that keeps lobbying for an increase in aid without focusing on the delivery mechanism. Increasing aid without changing the delivery mechanisms and rules is not going to have any more impact on the poor. Current levels of aid could be made at least 20 or 30 times more effective. And that should be our first task, because without fundamental reform of the aid system in the United States and elsewhere, outcomes in terms of equity and opportunity for the poor will not improve.

Rules and regulations from the 1940s are not suitable for the 21st century context. America cannot claim to be the center of global competitiveness and the home of a vibrant private sector while simultaneously creating a security development complex that captures its aid. The United States is not anomalous in this regard. Most global aid, to various degrees, is captured by contracting firms. Therefore, the global rules that support this complex and prevent the creation of functioning states and functioning markets on the ground need fundamental rethinking. Witnessing the security development complex in action has led most non-governmental organizations and civil society groups working in developing countries to advocate the doctrine of "do no harm" as the first rule. Isn't this sad, that our first rule of business now should be to preach to ourselves that we should do no harm, while continuously documenting that we are actually doing harm?

Civil society and universities here, the social organisms that underpin the vibrancy of the American middle class, need to be brought into this debate in particular. Unless these issues become issues of public discussion, they will remain marginal, and the effect will be the perpetuation of the current inefficiencies. After all, aid comes from taxes, and taxes are part of the social contract of the obligations and rights of citizenship. Hurricane Katrina showed that these failures are not confined to foreign aid operations. These implementation issues are as significant domestically as they are internationally, and they will only persist as environmental problems continue.

In a world that is one degree warmer, the western United States could once again be plagued by perennial droughts, devastating agricultural output, and the driving out of human habitation on an unprecedented scale. In a world that is two degrees warmer, in the southeastern United States, lower summer rainfall and soaring temperatures could slash sorghum and soybean production in half. In a world that is six degrees warmer, the entire global population might be living with, or dying, as a result of issues such as ocean stratification and hydrogen sulfide poisoning. Our global systems are of human making, but not of human design. The future is becoming more difficult, so the more we postpone action, the greater the problem. We must be proactive rather than reactive, and the entire nature of public policy now needs to be geared towards coherence. This in turn requires a medium and long-term view as an issue of design. The consequences if we do not start thinking in this way are almost too devastating to imagine.

In the past, public policy has assumed that the future is either benign or improving. Today, with the environment, we don't have that luxury. We need to think about the consequences of our actions now and rethink the nature of public consensus and action, vis a vis 20 years ahead of time. Waiting to react, as Katrina showed, is only going to have devastating results. The global poor are the most vulnerable to the threats emanating from food, security,

# AMERICAN AID HAS BEEN CAPTURED BY A DEVELOPMENT SECURITY COMPLEX THAT IS STRONGLY ENTRENCHED TO A POWERFUL SET OF INTEREST GROUPS, SUCH AS SHIPPING AND AGRICULTURAL LOBBYING, NGOS, AND CONGRESS.

and environmental issues. Not only do we need to focus on the relationship between short and medium term action in these realms more consciously, we also need to map backwards from our shared future objective to today's organizational constraints and deduce how best to remove these constraints.

This requires concerted action at the local, national, regional and global levels. As John Dewey once remarked, "Only continuous inquiry, continuous in the sense of being connected as well as persistent, can provide the material of enduring opinion of our public matters." Because these issues are global, the public that is affected by them is global. One of the most significant challenges for us now is how to exercise public power. If we are to tackle the key challenges of our times, we must reach a consensus on the role of national and international public institutions in the 21st century.

In his Lowell lecture of 1989, Jean Mayer concluded, "We need a change in priorities, a conversion, if you believe with me that greater knowledge brings greater responsibility. We have the knowledge and have very little excuse."

This plea for a change in priorities has never been more pertinent. The aid syndrome is part of a pathology and, like any pathology, needs reform. But reform cannot come without debate through public discussion. Only in this way can the disconnect between theory and practice be overcome. Universities, particularly distinguished ones such as Tufts, cannot be ivory towers. I know that programs like EPIIC are not attempts at being ivory towers, but rather attempts to be in the world and to change it. They have to be part of the vibrant tissue of debate and discussion and provide the ground for the formulation of alternatives to present reality. Dealing with causes rather than symptoms requires a major focus on institutional design, and the nature of public power is central to this.

Our view of public power has to change from an instrument of constraint to a tool for enabling the achievement of collective objectives and aspirations. We live in an interconnected world, and we cannot tackle global issues in isolation. The clash of civilizations can only be a self-fulfilling prophecy. To avoid this requires revisiting the design of international organizations and aid, and the United States must play a central role in this process. Honoring Jean Mayer is a way for us to engage with both the enduring challenges that he was cognizant of and the enduring legacy of hope that he has left us with. Human agency is and can be the major instrument of global reform. We must change our minds and reorder our priorities. Our survival depends on it.

Excerpts from the question and answer session

Laura Kaplan, sophomore
When you were speaking of the farmers in Afghanistan and their ability to compete with farmers in the United States because of subsidies given by the United States government, I couldn't help but think that in the *New York Times* recently there has been a focus on Afghanistan regarding opium. Do you think the focus in Afghanistan on the opium trade is a result of lack of opportunity in other farming markets?

A.G.
Thank you for the question. First of all it's not just the United States. The European Union has the largest amount of subsidies for extremely ineffective farmers. My first point is a level playing field. The World Bank and IMF would not lend to any country that subsidized its agriculture and dismantled half of the agriculture in Africa on the basis of that doctrine. Look at peanuts in Senegal, or other sets of activities. If it makes such good economic sense that the poorest countries should not engage in that practice, what is the justification for the richest countries? So my first point is about creating a level playing field. Either economics is national and actually subordinate to a political economy of power in a consensus, or it's a science. Currently, it is not a science; it's an art. Second, in 2002 (in Afghanistan) opium was rare. Food aid became a driver of opium. The current food subsidy policy is that the United States will only give food assistance in kind. It refuses to provide food assistance in cash. What's the difference? If you provided food assistance in cash, one, the cost of transport and administration would drop very significantly. It would signal to regional markets and national markets that food production domestically and regionally is critical to relief of emergencies. There is not a part of Afghanistan that you could not reach through the market mechanism. The issue was not the lack of access; the issue was lack of money to buy. We [Afghanistan] have known the market for a couple thousand years and yet we are being treated as though we were from the Stone Age and did not know how the market functioned.

Food companies, particularly wheat companies during the height of the Soviet Union, perfected the art of predicting harvests, because their future depended on it. How much the Soviet Union was going to buy was a critical driver of the foreign market. With that kind of technology, you could predict very reliably what the harvest would be and based on that could design a food distribution system to reinforce rather than destroy. What happened was the exact reverse. So this is the point about Mayer's point, we have the knowledge but we don't put it to use.

Now, regarding opium, there are two sets of issues. One is criminality. Twenty individuals in Afghanistan control the entire heroin trade. Not a single person in this country or in Europe or in any others is willing to name them or to take legal action against them. So one cannot practice both hypocrisy and cooperation. At the farm gate, the price of opium coming in is about $850 million to $1 billion per year. So it's a $24 billion industry, $22 billion of which is outside of Afghanistan. And every single nation along the way is involved. Why are we not focusing on the rest of the $22 billion? This is, again, the level playing field argument. The cost of heroin in London is cheaper than a cappuccino. It has dropped continuously every year over the last ten years.

Last point, the answer to opium is global market relationships. I could design a system here with scientists and a variety of experts to be able to get agricultural productivity to the level of industrial development. But the world has to make a choice. What's the choice? Legalize drugs, then opium becomes a commodity. And as any economist would tell you, Afghanistan would have no advantage in growing opium globally. There are hundreds of other places that could grow it better, and there'd be no demand. Why is that not being done? Because the politics of the middle class in this country (US) is not going to accept it. No politician is going to come out and stand up and run for election on the basis of legalization. If that is your political constraint, don't force me to cut the heads of the farmers there. We have to talk sense to each other. Here, there is politics as a constraint. There, it is no politics as a constraint. Alternatively, come with an economic design strategy that we think is necessary to get out of this. At $1,000 income per capita legally, there is no opium production. It doesn't make sense because it is back breaking work. So cotton will not compete with opium, but t-shirts will. Now the question is, will people be willing to create the conditions for the production of t-shirts?

Raoul Alwani, sophomore

I keep thinking about the example you used of how the WFP kind of messed up the food market. I don't think they would intentionally screw up the market. But after conflicts, maybe markets aren't running as well and people are in need of food but maybe they can't get it. How do you balance short-term needs with those in the long term?

A.G.

First, you're assuming the WFP is a functioning organization with accountability and transparency. Let me bring one thing to your attention, this is the same UN agency that refuses to provide audit reports to its Board of Governors. So its Board of Governors, the people who are providing the money, are actually not provided with the reports.

Secondly, organizational interests are now running wild. If you read the Oil-for-Food Inquiry, that's one of the most intense. The extent of corruption in running of food for aid becomes very clear. What is the nexus? Every single company in the developed countries and in the developing countries was involved in this scandal. So, corruption has become organized, it is not disorganized. Take another 5,000 pages of reports from the UN's own inspectors – I had to consider this because I was a candidate for becoming Secretary-General of the UN and I had to examine the materials. So we are dealing with an organized series of interests that do not have accountabilities. As citizens, we assume good intentions and say x amount of money has to go to humanitarian purposes because we have not thought through the problems of implementation. Implementation is messy, that's why it's not sexy. That's why the ivory tower does not teach it. You know what you are required to know at the World Bank, only how to operate the fund. There is not a single course on how to manage a project, nor is there one at the UN. It evolves. Everybody makes mistakes and they learn. Does formal economics give you the grounding for running a large scale project at the World Bank? No, but that is the type of recruitment the World Bank is doing. So there are lots of mistakes…What we now need to hold ourselves responsible for are the unintended consequences of policies that we practice. Because it's the result, not our intentions and this means really thinking from the objective backwards because now we know the patterns.

Austin Siadak, sophomore
In terms of the US Government not providing cash, was it based on the fungibility of monetary aid or deeper-seated economic and political interests within the bureaucracy itself?

A.G.
This is one area where someone from Boston, the former director of USAID Andrew Natsios, tried to break this nexus. He completely failed in Congress. The set of interests that have benefitted are enormous – the shipping lobby, the farming lobby and the NGOs. Unless the nexus is broken, it has nothing to do with fungibility.

Ina Breuer, Project on Justice in Times of Transition
You have been considered as both a candidate for Secretary-General of the United Nations and as head of the World Bank. From your perspective, what reform process do these institutions need to undergo?

A.G.
First of all, in terms of the UN, it will take ten years. It is really broken. The Secretary-General is far more Secretary than General. And that's the way it is designed. The beginning of the reform of the UN is going to begin from money. One thing that I learned from Max Weber that has been profoundly effective in my life is, he said that those who don't work need to

DISCOURSE

DO NO HARM?
THE SECURITY
DEVELOPMENT COMPLEX

ASHRAF GHANI

51

12 OF 12

# Rules and regulations from the 1940s are not suitable for the 21st century context.

be supported by others. He said follow the money. And it has been a remarkable guide. The core of it, $10 billion a year, now is spent on peacekeeping. And another $10 billion is spent on the rest of things. Gaining control and establishing the right mechanisms of account-ability is critical to reform. Second, it is a people's issue. The UN should be a global body that really recruits globally. Instead, recruitment in the UN is one of the most patronage-ridden sets of operations that the world has seen. The opportunity here is that close to 30 percent of the UN staff is going to retire in the next four years. I would spend easily – if I was in charge of global policy – $100 million dollars to buy the current staff of the UN out and begin fresh. The current staff did not reach out to this generation. When it could have made one of the most significant alliances of development, where the brightest minds of the world, based on competitive recruitment, are made to understand, both theoretically and directly, consummate poverty, it didn't. It should be a badge of honor, and they should live on the front lines for six months to a year so that theory and practice are really combined and a community develops where the major preparation for working at the UN takes place.

Then it's selectivity. I would abolish most of the UN agencies overnight and focus on three to four key issues. The model of technical assistance was a 1945 conception – that every single thing can be done through tech assistance. Five million dollars a year goes to technical assistance in Africa to employ 60,000 people from developing countries to write the reports for people in developed countries that no one is going to read. Accountability does not come through reporting in that manner.

In terms of the World Bank, the core issue is that there are about 100 countries that require assistance during the next 20-30 years. And one needs to be able to think about the economic system as a design issue, not as an issue of doctrine, and really connect and acquire the set of capabilities for these countries. That requires a complete set of capabil-ities that one can use to work across development security to bring a holistic perspective. When I became Finance Minister, I wanted to build a functioning ministry, not one in my image. I asked the World Bank and the IMF two questions: What should the ministry of finance do? What should it not do? It took them six months and they came back with a series of dysfunctional case studies. They did not have the knowledge.

/ END

# A BATTL OVER MINES AND MINDS

HANNAH
FLAMM

Hannah Flamm graduated from Tufts in February 2009 with a degree in Political Science. She is a member of the inaugural class of Synaptic Scholars and a co-founder of the Poverty and Power Research Initiative at the Institute for Global Leadership, Tufts University. Hannah has been traveling to El Salvador since 2004. In 2007, she began researching gold mining with another Tufts student, Maia Kolchin-Miller, and a grant from the Anne E. Borghesani Memorial Prize of the Tufts International Relations Program. The project evolved into the joint fact-finding proposal with support from the Institute for Global Leadership; the Massachusetts Institute of Technology-US Geological Survey Science Impact Collaborative (MUSIC); the Tufts Water: Systems, Science and Society (WSSS) graduate program; and the Consensus Building Institute in Washington, D.C.

Introduction

"The gold mine at El Dorado will use 10.4 liters of water per second. That is almost 900,000 liters a day, what a family would consume over twenty years," reads a local anti-mining pamphlet. One anti-mining leader in the municipality of San Isidro explained, "The mining would occur where the country's main water reserves are located. Half the population of San Salvador gets its water from the *Río Lempa*. It is life for us, and it would be contaminated if the mines open." Another representative of the mining opposition asked me, "Would you accept a new industry that brings contamination to the water, the soil, the air? Mining pollutes with heavy metals, cyanide, mercury, and other poisons. This mining company, Pacific Rim, would use two tons of cyanide per day, over seven thousand tons in a decade, at El Dorado. We live here. We have to think of our children. How could we accept this?"

The mining companies, and the industry's supporters in government, the private sector, and rural communities, argue that the development of a gold mining industry in El Salvador would produce economic development. They argue the industry offers financial investment, desperately needed in the impoverished northern portion of the country where the mine projects are concentrated; job opportunities; and additional, significant social and infrastructural investments. Over the past two years, the mining companies operating in El Salvador financed a major "green mining" media campaign in which they insisted that new technology and environmental standards obviate the environmental concerns of the opposition. Pacific Rim's website highlights that the company is "setting industry standards for environmental stewardship and social responsibility."

El Salvador is the last country in Central America to resurrect its gold mining industry since the low global gold prices in the 1950s and the region's Cold War-era civil wars prompted the industry's decline. In the 1990s, under pressure from the World Bank, El Salvador and other Central American countries reformed their mining laws to attract greater investment: Honduras in 1991, El Salvador and Nicaragua in 1996, and Guatemala in 1997. In each case, the reforms made the metallic resources available for purchase with reduced financial and regulatory burdens on potential investors. In El Salvador, the National Legislative Assembly reduced annual royalty rates from four percent to two percent of corporate revenue. Guatemala's shrunk from six percent to one percent.

According to Pacific Rim, if its three main Salvadoran mine sites were to open, the company would become the biggest taxpayer in El Salvador.

Prompted by the significant rise in metal commodity prices, around a dozen gold mining companies have appeared in El Salvador in the past fifteen years, sparking a vocal anti-mining movement. Operating at the local and national level, the individuals and organizations involved in the opposition movement are primarily concerned with the potential environmental, economic, and social effects of mining. They strongly distrust the foreign mining companies and, perhaps more importantly, distrust their own government to protect their interests and needs.

The debate over whether or not to allow gold mines to open has taken place in this atmosphere of suspicion, fear, confrontation, and distrust – and in the context of an electoral campaign. On March 15, 2009, El Salvador held its fourth national presidential elections since the 1992 Peace Accords. For the first time, the left-wing party, the Farabundo Martí National Liberation Front (FMLN), established out of the wartime peasant-based guerrilla movement, won 51.27 percent of the vote to the right-wing Nationalist Republican Alliance (ARENA) party's 48.72 percent. Evidently, the country is still deeply divided.

In the halls of the National Legislative Assembly, many of the FMLN offices are decorated with red bumper stickers reading "*No a la minería, Sí a la vida*" (No to mining, yes to life). El Salvador's outgoing president, Elías Antonio "Tony" Saca, and ARENA generally, have been much more hesitant than the FMLN to take a firm stand on mining, because any position could have become a liability in the elections. (In the last weeks of the campaign, perhaps as a political strategy, President Saca did make an unequivocal statement against mining, "Not even one mine exploitation permit will be granted while [I am] the president. Not even the environmental permission, which precedes the permission granted by the Ministry of Economy, will be granted."[1])

However, what has resulted as the government's greatest liability is not its position on mining, but its inaction. In December 2008, Pacific Rim El Salvador, the largest investor of all the companies operating in El Salvador, sued the Salvadoran government for $600 million under the Central American Free Trade Agreement (CAFTA). The case is based on the government's failure to obey its own regulations, which stipulate that the Ministry of Environment and Ministry of Economy must respond to a company's application for a mining exploitation concession within 60 days. It has been five years since Pacific Rim applied.

Between 2007 and 2008, I visited El Salvador on three occasions to explore the mining debate. I met with the leaders of the opposition movement, observing their community information sessions and the organization of protest activities. I visited Pacific Rim's El Dorado mine site and field offices, accompanied by the company's chief executives. I interviewed lawyers; scientists; religious leaders; journalists; national and local politicians across the political spectrum; and community members located near several proposed mine sites.

In 2008, with support from Tufts University, the Massachusetts Institute of Technology, and the Consensus Building Institute, and after consultation with Pacific Rim, anti-mining movement leaders, and the University of Central America in San Salvador, I attempted to carry out a stakeholder assessment to gather independent data on local stakeholders' positions on mining.

The assessment, the first part of "joint fact-finding," one of the emerging best practices in environmental conflict negotiation meant to integrate hard, scientific data with local values and knowledge, would map the local population's primary questions and concerns as well as their level of interest in a permanent stakeholder engagement forum. If Pacific Rim's flagship El Dorado mine were to open and a critical mass of people endorsed the proposed forum, the mechanism would aim to create the neutral, legitimate space for community representatives, Pacific Rim, local government, and independent scientists to negotiate, in an inclusive and ongoing manner, terms of the mining operations; methods to increase, and distribute fairly, the benefits of mining; and remediation or compensation measures for environmental or other damages.

The assessment was never carried out. At the peak of the opposition movement's most militant actions, when anti-mining organizers burned $30,000 worth of Pacific Rim's machinery, rumors spread that I worked for Pacific Rim and

# "WE FOUGHT OVER A DECADE FOR THIS LAND WITH OUR BLOOD. OUR BROTHERS, PARENTS, AND CHILDREN DIED HERE. WE WON'T HAND IT OVER NOW WITHOUT A FIGHT."

I lost all credibility. Days after I left, on July 4, 2008, Pacific Rim, the last mining company in El Salvador, also left.

Few major players in El Salvador appear willing to negotiate or compromise on the mining issue. This article, based on my research and these interactions, is a story not only about mining, but also about a country constrained by high levels of political polarization and social and institutional distrust. Neither the foreign companies nor the opposition movement could achieve its goals through current Salvadoran government channels.

## Pacific Rim and El Dorado

Pacific Rim El Salvador is a wholly owned subsidiary of Pacific Rim Mining Corporation, based in Vancouver, Canada. Since purchasing the rights to El Dorado, located in the municipality of San Isidro, in 2002, the company has spent over $44 million in El Salvador. Pacific Rim has other less developed mine sites in El Salvador and partial ownership at operations outside the country as well. The Denton-Rawhide residual heap leach gold operation in Nevada was a major source of cash flow, until the company sold its rights there in late 2008.[2]

The El Dorado project, designed to be a one quarter-square mile, hard rock, subterranean mine, is one of around two dozen gold exploration projects in northern El Salvador. It is located approximately 40 miles east of the capital, in the department of Cabañas. Spanning 700 square miles and with a population just over 150,000, Cabañas is by many measures the poorest of the country's fourteen departments. In 2002, average per capita income in rural Cabañas was $1,676, compared to the national rural average of $2,579 and the national urban average of $7,124. Average life expectancy is 62 years in rural Cabañas, almost ten years less than the national average. Approximately 42 percent of the department's population does not have access to potable water, while nationally only 26 percent lack access.[3] The majority of the population near Pacific Rim's property is subsistence farmers.

Since receiving its exploration license, Pacific Rim has submitted Environmental Impact Assessments, conducted pre-feasibility studies, held public consultations, and updated its resource estimates. In 2004, Pacific Rim applied for an exploitation permit to begin the production phase at the mine. The permit would allow for a six-year operation with a production average of 80,000 ounces of gold per year, though during an interview in June 2007, Pacific Rim's CEO and President Thomas Shrake remarked, "This is only the start." Subsequent exploration work indicated Pacific Rim could increase its operation to 150,000-ounce annual production for ten years. The January 2008 estimate found that the El Dorado mine held 1.4 million ounces of gold (and 7.4 million ounces of silver).

Ultimately, with further exploration, Pacific Rim expects El Dorado to produce up to five million ounces of gold in total. This is not a trivial sum when the value of the dollar is low and the price of gold correspondingly high. In 2007, when the price of gold circled around $650 per ounce, El Dorado was estimated to be worth $3.3 billion.[4] The global price of gold topped $1,000 per ounce in early March 2009, as fears of the global financial crisis continued to deepen.[5]

According to Pacific Rim, if its three main Salvadoran mine sites were to open, the company would become the biggest taxpayer in El Salvador. Operations at El Dorado alone are expected to produce $20 million in taxes each year. With other mining companies extracting the 15 to 25 million ounces of gold that El Salvador allegedly holds nationally, the industry could increase gross domestic product by 1.4 percent and exports by 20.8 percent over the next 20 years.[6]

At the local level, Pacific Rim argues that its financial, social, and infrastructural investment would have an immensely positive effect. Its operations would provide hundreds of direct and indirect jobs. With Pacific Rim's taxes and royalty payments, the annual budget for the municipality of San Isidro would jump from around $100,000 to around $1 million. (When Tom Shrake invited me to meet with the mayor of San Isidro, Juan Ignacio Bautista, the mayor highlighted the "good communication" and "sincere relationship" that his office had developed with the company.) In 2002, the annual tax income for the entire department of Cabañas, which holds nine municipalities including San Isidro, was under $1.3 million.[7] During El Dorado's exploration phase, when a company makes smaller expenditures than after the mine opens, Pacific Rim spent almost $1 million per year on community projects. To the villagers, Pacific Rim's donations are basic necessities: fertilizer subsidies, sheet metal roofs, medical services, school supplies. To the company, the goods are the means to a "social license to operate."

In terms of environmental impact, Pacific Rim executives charge that the mining opposition, "poorly informed, ideological and politically motivated," exaggerates the potential for harm. Company representatives argue that agriculture and raising livestock can coexist with mining. They allege their operations would not affect the local water supply because they would use only rainwater collected during the rainy season and water pumped up from the old El Dorado mine that was shut down in the early 1950s. The water would be recycled and discharged into the local supply after purification and monitoring.

Contamination from cyanide and acid mine drainage would not be problems at El Dorado, company representatives say. The risk from cyanide use "is manageable" and cyanide is used in many other, non-controversial industrial processes. Its transportation, processing, and storage would be strictly regulated. The company plans to line the tailings pond, which holds the mine operation's toxic waste, with two impermeable layers for extra protection against accidental or incremental seepage.

Pacific Rim executives say that the risk of acid mine drainage would be negligible because the rock at El Dorado contains very little sulfide minerals, the key ingredient for the manufacture of sulfuric acid. They say that the gold at El Dorado is of such high quality that only 3.5 tons of rock would be extracted to produce one ounce of gold. (To yield 150,000 ounces of gold annually for a decade, over five million tons of waste rock would need storage.) Pacific Rim claims that all land removed during mining will be restored with the mine's closure.

In interviews, the company's executives argued that their operations would actually help to fix some of the region's existing environmental problems. More and cleaner water would flow in the local streams with the monitored discharge from the mines' operations. The thousands of trees that the company would plant would help counter the region's deforestation. With their greenhouse, re-vegetation, and erosion prevention efforts, "this place may look better post-mining than it does today," one executive said.

According to Pacific Rim, only a minority of Salvadorans opposes mining. The company and the two major national newspapers, *La Prensa Gráfica* and *El Diario de Hoy*, often cite a survey of 1,800 Salvadorans from across the country, published in January 2008 by *Métodos Estudios y Procesos* (MEP), which found that 67 percent of respondents support mining projects, either "managed responsibly" or "unlimited," and that only 30 percent were in favor of banning all mining in El Salvador. The demographic breakdown showed youth, the rural population, and citizens of lower socio-economic strata are greater supporters of mining than their elderly, urban, and more well off counterparts. MEP reports the results showed no trends based on political affiliation or ideology.[8]

While mining is an issue of national importance, many Salvadorans who live far from the proposed mine sites are less informed about mining – and have less at stake – than those living in the northern zone of the country. Thus the

MEP survey results may be skewed by its nation-wide population sample. Moreover, even substantial portions of Salvadorans living near the proposed mine sites lack information about mining. One survey, published in January 2008 by the University Institute of Public Opinion of the University of Central America in El Salvador, interviewed 1,256 residents of northern El Salvador. The results showed that only 20 percent of respondents were "aware of the existence of mining projects in their municipality" and 30 percent of these respondents did not know its name.[9] When I asked one interviewee in San Isidro her opinion on gold mining, she responded, "Mining has been going on here for years, and it has not hurt us yet." The woman, who lives less than 100 meters from the terrain Pacific Rim had designated for its 634,000-cubic meter tailings pond, most likely imagined that the company's exploration drilling was the mining itself.

## The Opposition Movement

The first organizing against mining in El Salvador began in Chalatenango, a department to the northwest of Cabañas on the border with Honduras. Several Canadian companies and their Salvadoran subsidiaries – Aura Silver Resources, Tribune Resources, Au Martinique, Intrepid Minerals, and Triada – had been exploring the region unbeknownst to the local population. Residents first discovered the presence of the companies in September 2005. The story, as told by members of the opposition movement, opens with a villager checking on his cattle. He notices his fences cut and men with backpacks walking around his land. The villager asks the men what they are doing. "Looking for mines," they said. The villager replies that all the mines were cleared out with the Peace Accords, thinking the men were looking for land mines. "No, no, gold and silver mines," the backpacked men explained.

The villager promptly informed community leaders. The companies began talking to community members. They apologized for their secretive entrance and paid for minor damages. They sought support from local religious and political leaders and attended meetings the communities called.

Two of the twelve-year civil war's legacies in Chalatenango, then a guerrilla stronghold, are strong community organization and symbolic value attached to land. When the mining issue arose, community development groups, which had evolved from the remnants of guerrilla organizations, worked quickly. They garnered support from government and church authorities, neighboring communities, and international solidarity organizations. The community groups effectively framed mining as a land rights issue. One interviewee explained to me, "We fought over a decade for this land with our blood. Our brothers, parents, and children died here. We won't hand it over now without a fight." Even children I spoke with in Chalatenango were adamantly anti-mining.

The local communities coordinated an effort to remove the companies' exploration markers. They planned protest marches, including one trek to place a larger-than-life, wooden Virgin Mary atop a mountain where companies had planned to mine. The national media started paying attention to mining. On two occasions, the communities organized successful roadblocks to prevent the entrance of the companies' executives. By 2007, after attempting to enter under as many as three different names, the Canadian companies and subsidiaries retreated from Chalatenango.

El Salvador is approximately 20,000 square kilometers, roughly the size of Rhode Island, and overpopulated with six million inhabitants (369 people per square kilometer).

They did not sell their property, leaving open the possibility of returning, but currently the companies have reinvested in Guatemala and Costa Rica.

The anti-mining movement in Chalatenango is not representative of the movement in other parts of the country. Cabañas, for example, is not as cohesive in terms of its position on mining, general politics, or its historical narrative. Today, the opposition movement is composed primarily of small rural organizations and national environmental or development organizations. Oxfam America is an active participant in the National Coalition on Metallic Mining, formed in 2005, and the FMLN is supportive of the movement. The governmental National Development Commission, the national Human Rights Ombudsman, and the Catholic Church have all made public statements against mining. According to Pacific Rim's executives, in the months after May 2007, when El Salvador's National Episcopal Conference formally pronounced its opposition to mining, the value of Pacific Rim's stock dropped 30-40 percent.

The opposition movement counts among its supporters the former Minister of Environment and Natural Resources, Hugo Barrera, and current Minister Carlos Guerrero. Barrera, vice president of ARENA's National Executive Council and owner of a giant snack-food company, came out publicly against mining in June 2006. In December 2006, Guerrero, a former Vice Minister of Public Works and owner of a construction company, replaced Barrera. Two years later, in July 2008, Guerrero is quoted in the online newspaper, *El Faro*, saying, "Mining is an industry that demands four times more energy than the average industry. The quantities of water resources it demands are industrial-size, *grandísimas*, which definitely has an impact on the environment."

The anti-mining network has international advocates as well. In February 2007, a letter drafted by U.S. and Canadian solidarity organizations, such as US-El Salvador Sister Cities, Community in Solidarity with the People of El Salvador (CISPES), SHARE El Salvador, and many others, and signed by 41 members of the U.S. House of Representatives pushed President Saca not to approve mining. The letter argued that mining could threaten El Salvador's Compact with the Millennium Challenge Account (MCA), an innovative U.S. foreign aid program that conditions assistance on good governance, effective poverty reduction measures, and, among other things, environmental stewardship. The $460 million MCA aid package – a grant paramount to an international political and financial "stamp of approval" – is designed to address poverty in the same northern third of El Salvador where mining would take place.

The main reasons the anti-mining movement opposes the industry's development are its environmental, economic, and social risks. While the most well-versed anti-mining activists can run through the list of contaminants mining would use or produce (aluminum, ammonia, antimony, arsenic, cadmium, chrome, cobalt, cyanide, iron, lead, mercury, nickel, nitrate, selenium, sulfate, and uranium), many supporters of the opposition movement sum up their position with the phrase: "*Vivo sin oro, pero no sin agua*" (I can live without gold, but not without water).

Environmental Risks

The 2008 University of Central America (UCA) public opinion survey found that, for the 62.5 percent of respondents against mining, the most common reason for opposition was the country's small geographical area.[10] El Salvador is approximately 20,000 square kilometers, roughly the size of Rhode Island, and overpopulated with six million inhabitants (369 people per square kilometer). The opposition movement argues it would be impossible to mine far from people. They say that the industry's potential negative effects would be exacerbated by the mine's inevitably close proximity to people and key natural resources.

The second most common reason for opposition to mining in the UCA survey was that mining would contaminate the environment, particularly water resources (21.9 percent). Pacific Rim's Environmental Impact Assessment reports that their operations at El Dorado would use 10.4 liters of water per second. They also do not trust the company to only take this water from rain and the shutdown 1950s mine. They do not trust the company to purify the water before returning it to the streams. Ultimately, they do not trust that the company will report honestly on their water consumption or environmental damage – or their ore extraction, profits, tax payments or anything else.

In March 2008, one of Pacific Rim's 600 exploration boreholes accidentally hit an aquifer in one village in San Isidro, cutting off several dozen families' water supply from natural springs and streams. The company immediately began trucking and piping in water and continued to do so until the natural sources returned two months later, in the rainy season. In the days following the accident, Pacific Rim sent its community liaisons to explain the accident and negotiate compensation with the village. But the liaisons did not work with the elected village leadership; instead they negotiated with a few families, known to favor mining and to be close with the mayor.

Predictably, this incident further alienated and infuriated community members opposed to mining and brought many more families to their side. "The borehole was six centimeters in diameter," one community leader fumed. "Look at the damage it did. If the mines open, they will build tunnels big enough for trucks to drive through them. You think that won't do damage?"

The piped water was allegedly too hot and dirty to drink; it made small animals die when they drank it. At least two other residents from the same village made public statements that natural springs on their land had also dried up in the past year. They reported that they had been afraid to say anything before and that Pacific Rim had compensated them financially for the damage and to close the issue. The pressure at this time on the community government threatened to dissolve it. For years, the government had been divided on how to react to Pacific Rim's presence; now they felt impotent with the company's failure to recognize or speak with them. The dry streambeds and empty water collection tanks were featured on the front pages of the national newspapers.

In numerous interviews, anti-mining activists noted that even without mining, El Salvador is experiencing water scarcity and environmental degradation through deforestation and industrial and agricultural pollution. Many interviewees in Cabañas asked, "How could we destroy our environment further?" Another interviewee, Dr. Norman Quijano, then an ARENA party deputy in the National Assembly serving on the Committee on Environment and Public Health, and now, as of January 2009, mayor-elect of San Salvador, drew an alternative conclusion. "If they suggested mining in the west of the country, where there are volcanoes, forests, and lots of tourism, I would say no. But in Morazán, Chalatenango, and Cabañas – it is already deforested there. I would not throw out that option." One Pacific Rim executive was of a similar mind. "About 90 percent of El Salvador is already deforested. Farmers deforest, and their fertilizers are contaminants. Why are people so worried about the tiny amount of land that mining would use?"

Inevitably, mining would alter the landscape and ecosystem by building roads, truck ramps, underground tunnels, ventilation systems, a processing plant, and tailings pond. The ore extraction and transportation involve big machinery, explosives, large quantities of water, and carry the potential for accidents, above and under ground, and the build up of sediment, fuel waste, and greases. At the processing plant, the extracted ore is turned to powder and mixed with lime and sodium cyanide to increase pH levels and dissolve the precious metals, respectively. Zinc is added to separate out the gold from the muddy slush; then sulfuric acid is added to remove the zinc. The remaining wastewater is sent to a plant for INCO treatment, a common procedure to oxidize the cyanide and make the wastewater more than 90 percent less toxic. The wastewater then remains in the tailings pond or gets recycled through the system before its ultimate discharge into the environment, in this case a decade or more after the mine closes, according to Pacific Rim.

The impact on vegetation, aquatic life, and animals could affect not only the environment and the economy, but also human health. The anti-mining movement is quick to show pictures and tell stories of skin rashes, allergies, respiratory diseases, chronic illnesses, cancers, and deaths linked to mining in other countries in Latin America and Africa with developed mining industries.

## Economic and Social Concerns

Anti-mining activists challenge Pacific Rim's and other companies' claim that mining will lead to development and economic growth for El Salvador. Mining is not a major economic force in Central America. In 2006, "mining and quarrying," which comprises metallic mining and nonmetallic industries such as fossil fuels, sand, gravel, and cement, accounted for less than 0.4 percent of El Salvador's GDP.[11] The figure was only slightly higher in Guatemala (0.6 percent) and Honduras (1.5 percent). Even with the expansion of the gold mining industry, these figures would not increase significantly, according to Oxfam.[12] By comparison, in El Salvador, the service and manufacturing sectors represented 54.5 percent and 21.4 percent of GDP in 2006, respectively. Agriculture contributed 9.0 percent of GDP. All of these sectors pale relative to the volume of remittances. In 2004, remittances were approximately as great as all export earnings in Guatemala and Honduras; in El Salvador, remittances were 70 percent greater than all export earnings.

The economic benefits of the mining industry are often short-lived, concentrated, and unpredictable. According to Oxfam's analysis of mining in Central America, Goldcorp's San Martin gold mine in Honduras, which opened in 2001, was already undergoing reclamation efforts by 2007.[13] Pacific Rim's El Dorado mine project is estimated to last six years, though subsequent estimates increased that figure as well as the company's annual production target, making it difficult to predict the probable lifespan of the mine. Unless the company's investments can be institutionalized and translated into other services and goods, the direct benefits of mining are few once the jobs dry up. Most skills Pacific Rim employees would learn are not transferable, though the company has made a serious effort to offer literacy classes to employees and potential employees.

The profits of mining are concentrated on several levels. Salvadoran law puts royalty rates at two percent of corporate revenue; in 2007, Pacific Rim estimated two percent would amount to $1-2 million. (The anti-mining activists are quick to argue the company is running off with 98 percent of the wealth. Pacific Rim executives explained in an interview that 50 percent of their revenue would go to employee salaries, buying land, and operating costs; 25 percent would go to taxes; the last 25 percent would be profit, half of which they would reinvest in the mine.) El Salvador's 1996 mining law stipulates that the central government and municipal government where the mine site is located split royalty payments evenly. In a June 2007 interview, Bautista, the mayor of San Isidro, described how he would spend this money. "Twenty five percent will go to administration: air conditioning, our employees, and other things for the office. The communities in the municipality will determine how to spend the rest. They have great need for electricity, potable water, and roads."

Bautista is known for his corruption. He regularly excludes villages in his municipality not supportive of his ARENA party from infrastructural projects. He withholds agricultural subsidies from individuals who do not support him. During the January 2009 national municipal and legislative elections, voting was suspended in San Isidro because so many Hondurans voted. Allegedly, Bautista facilitated their transportation and paid each person as much as $100 to vote for him. When the vote was rescheduled the following week, Bautista won his fourth consecutive three-year term in office.

The benefits of mining are also concentrated at the level of employment. In 2007, Pacific Rim employed 150 local Salvadorans. San Isidro has a population of 14,000 and the department has 150,000 residents. While the number of Pacific Rim's employees could double for several years if El Dorado were to open, the later phases of the mine operation require fewer workers.

The economic benefits of mining are unpredictable because of volatility in world markets and the boom-bust cycle in gold commodity prices. Moreover, in El Salvador, and many other countries, a mine's potential economic benefit, and environmental impact, are calculated based on a company's estimate of mineral reserves to be mined. The companies are not bound to these estimates, and, regardless of their accuracy, it is the price of gold that determines how much a company mines. "If the price of gold were to double, it is very common for a pit to get two to three times as big," explained Dr. Robert Moran, a hydro-geologist based in Colorado who has analyzed Pacific Rim's Environmental Impact Assessment as well as many others in Central America and around the world. The expected profit affects the size of the mine, its lifespan, and the extraction techniques, which, in turn affect the actual profit and environmental impact.

In addition to the commodity price variable issue, uncertainty in the mining industry arises because companies tend to begin operating a mine before conducting a full mineral resource estimate. They often choose to do further drill explorations only after entering the production phase, when the company has a stronger cash flow. This practice is legal and economical from the company's perspective, but it means that its initial estimates are prone to change once mining begins. Meanwhile, the government grants the extraction concessions based on the company's initial estimates.

Dr. Moran noted the imprudence of trusting technical predictions and computer simulations. He compared this methodology utilized for granting mining licenses to that of the US insurance industry. The insurance industry is "one of the richest industries in the US. And they would never ask you to predict whether you're going to have an accident. They would look at the statistics of twenty-year-olds getting into accidents and charge insurance based on that."

Financial assurance laws could mitigate the uncertainty involved in the mining industry. In the US and Canada, the laws oblige mining companies to "guarantee that future environmental costs will be paid for (both during operation and after mine closure), even if the company goes bankrupt."[14] In other words, "medium and long-term environmental costs are internalized within the operating costs of the companies." Without such laws in El Salvador, the people would likely end up paying for damages.

The opposition is also concerned with the social ramifications of the mine operations and its accompanying influx of wealth. Most directly, mining will displace people. Pacific Rim's exploration work is spread throughout villages, sometimes so close that several interviewees said that while the noisy drill rigs were located near their homes, they could not even hear their television sets. The opposition is also concerned with increases in the cost of goods, labor, property, taxes, and water. Often, in the areas surrounding mine sites, prostitution, alcohol consumption, and crime increase. The local gap in income and wealth tends to grow. While the government could theoretically design policies and programs to reduce these negative ramifications, the opposition movement cites significant evidence demonstrating that it is unlikely their mayors would have the capacity or will to do so.

Scarcity of Independent Information

An overriding problem with the mining debate in El Salvador is that almost all of its information comes from either the companies or the opposition movement. Dr. Moran's October 2005 review of Pacific Rim's Environmental Impact Assessment (EIA) provided one independent, technical perspective on El Dorado, although he was commissioned by the Association for Economic and Social Development,

One Pacific Rim executive was of a similar mind. "About 90 percent of El Salvador is already deforested. Farmers deforest, and their fertilizers are contaminants. Why are people so worried about the tiny amount of land that mining would use?"

an organization now active in the anti-mining movement in Cabañas. His main findings were that the EIA "lacks basic testing and data necessary to adequately define baseline water quantity and quality conditions" and that "the public EIA review process is clearly lacking in openness and transparency." The EIA is 1,400 pages long, portions on cyanide management are in English only, and only one copy of it was available for public review and comment for only ten working days.[15]

For the most part, neither the public nor the government has responded to Dr. Moran's criticisms. In an interview, Pacific Rim's CEO and President Thomas Shrake described Dr. Moran's Technical Review as a "cookie sheet" report by someone "paid to condemn mining projects." But Shrake did grant that "the hydro-geologic data was a little light" in the company's first EIA. "We should have done more at the beginning to prove our conclusions, but they are so simple we did not want to spend money on it," he explained. Pacific Rim did go back to do more hydro-geologic testing. Shrake say that the results do not change their original conclusions. Still, this information is not provided by independent, widely trusted sources.

A former Minister of Finance, Manuel Enrique Hinds, who oversaw El Salvador's conversion from the Salvadoran *colón* to the US dollar in 2001, wrote another allegedly independent report on mining. It was published in June 2007, entitled "Gold Mining in El Salvador: Costs and Benefits," and could easily be mistaken for a report written by Pacific Rim. Its cover is an idyllic, sun-lit forest scene, and the header on every other page is "The Economic Benefits of Gold Mining in El Salvador." The tone, arguments, and statistics, which are hardly distinguishable from those Pacific Rim uses elsewhere, and the six pages on environmental impacts, which dismisses each of the concerns, add to that general impression. The report's conclusion is: "To not permit gold mining in the country would be to reject very important benefits for some risks that can be reduced to levels lower than many other activities currently permitted in the country."[16]

According to an Oxfam report, Hinds' analysis is faulty, as well as biased: "Hinds hypothesizes that not only will El Dorado open, but that each year another mine will open, leading to 10 mines the size of the proposed El Dorado.... He also projects that new mines might continue to open annually indefinitely into the future."[17] Hinds uses a similar method to estimate the number of jobs the mines would generate (450 direct jobs, 2,500 additional jobs, and 36,000 jobs if three other mines like El Dorado were to open).

The Salvadoran government has made an effort to provide theoretically independent information, but thus far has produced nothing. In June 2007, the Minister of the Environment, Carlos Guerrero, said no mining permits would be granted until a Strategic Environmental Evaluation was conducted. The Evaluation was meant to consider the environmental, economic, and social viability of the mining industry and its cumulative impact on the northern zone of El Salvador. The 1998 Law of the Environment, which created the Ministry of Environment, mandates the Strategic Evaluation.

In June 2008, the Minister of Economy Yolanda Mayora de Gavidia allegedly began an international effort to raise the funds for the Evaluation. But Gavidia was replaced by the end of the month by Ricardo Esmahán, a businessman and former president of the Salvadoran Chamber of Agriculture and Agribusiness. Gavidia became general secretary of the Central American Secretariat for Economic Integration. The current status of the fundraising effort is not known publicly.

### Lack of Institutional and Social Trust

The lack of trust in Salvadoran society and towards the government is a result, in large part, of the country's history and political culture. Many members of the mining opposition, and supporters of the FMLN, are cynical towards the government. People see impunity and corruption as well as low levels of institutional independence and capacity. Many members of the opposition do not count on the government to protect their interests or offer legal recourse, should they need it. The general political polarization that has grown in the past decade and, in the case of mining, the power gap between multinational companies and small, rural organizations, contribute significantly to the lack of social trust. These factors greatly inhibit communication, rational debate, and the ability for either side to negotiate or compromise on mining.

Pacific Rim charges that the anti-mining movement is ideological, poorly informed, and politically motivated. The company contends that the movement inflates the risks associated with mining; does not compare mining-related risks to those of other existing, non-controversial industries; and does not take into account the protection that new technologies offer.

It is true that the opposition movement is not always careful with its arguments against mining. Anti-mining leaders compare open-pit mines in other Latin American and African countries to Pacific Rim's plans for a subterranean mine at El Dorado. Several anti-mining groups have organized trips to operational mines in Honduras and Guatemala so Salvadorans can see for themselves the social conflict, cyanide dust clouds, dried riverbeds, sick children, and dead land. Lead, mercury, and arsenic have been found at the Valle de Siria gold mine operated in Honduras by Goldcorp Inc. and its subsidiary Entre Mares. At the Marlin Mine in Guatemala, owned by Goldcorp and Glamis Gold, there have been violent clashes between the local population, largely opposed to the open-pit mine there, and security agents defending the companies' activities. The anti-mining groups and villagers return from these trips intent on conveying the disturbing truths they have found. As one person put it, "We are educating ourselves and looking out for our villages' and children's best interests." But as many of them travel with the certainty and sense of urgency that mining must be stopped, potentially critical nuances can slip by. The characteristics and effects of open pit mines differ from those of subterranean mines, for example. Still, the bigger-picture cause for concern may yet apply.

Neither mining companies nor the opposition movement see much flexibility in the other's position and, by necessity, each side has firm objectives of its own to pursue. Pacific Rim professes to be interested in talking to the anti-mining movement; they have held public meetings and participated in some debates and conferences. But ultimately, the company has an agenda to pursue on its shareholders' behalf. In interviews, Pacific Rim executives indicated they would be willing to negotiate the conditions under which mining takes place, within the boundary of what the law dictates; but it is difficult to negotiate like that with an opposition movement that fully rejects the development of the industry.

On the whole, the anti-mining movement is not interested in talking to Pacific Rim. Previously, representatives of the anti-mining movement did participate in forums with Pacific Rim and other companies, but now they do not see the benefit. From their perspective, the mining companies have not and will not respond to their demands or concerns. They even distrust people who communicate with "the enemy." One anti-mining leader said to me, "There is nothing to negotiate. Mining must be stopped. So why would you talk to the company? They will only trick you."

With its historical experience, political narrative, and limited resources, the anti-mining movement has found that it can best advance its cause with negative power: interrupting, protesting, and destroying. Opposition members are not taken seriously inside the National Assembly or Canadian Embassy, so they set up camp outside the buildings and in the *Plaza Cívica*. They cannot keep the companies from receiving exploration or exploitation permits, so they burn the company's property until the costs are too high for the company to maintain its presence – or, as the opposition leaders might put it, "until the companies learn their lesson." So far, the strategy has worked; after all, today, there is no mining in El Salvador. Still, the severely constrained communication and rational interaction could become disadvantages to both sides in the future, if the mines open.

One anti-mining leader said to me, "There is nothing to negotiate. Mining must be stopped. So why would you talk to the company? They will only trick you."

Reform of the Mining Law and Other Recent Developments

The National Assembly received a proposal to reform the national mining law in late 2006. The proposal, which would ban gold mining, was submitted by the Foundation for Studies of the Application of the Law (FESPAD), a member of the National Coalition on Metallic Mining. The Legislative Assembly never seriously considered the bill.

A year later, in November 2007, the center-right National Conciliation Party (PCN) submitted a proposal to facilitate mining. According to PCN deputy, Orlando Arévalo, also a member of the Inter-American Commission of Mines and Energy, the legal reform would increase royalty payments that companies must pay to the government. In an interview in June 2007, Arévalo said he believed in "finding a balance. Protect the environment and take advantage of our natural resources. Share the benefits between the company and the state. It is the new wave of win-win." After receiving the PCN proposal, the National Assembly created an Ad-Hoc Commission on Mining with members from all five political parties. The Commission closed in the spring of 2008 and has yet to issue its conclusions publicly.

By February 2008, the National Coalition on Metallic Mining was reporting on the PCN's proposal in the *Diario Co Latino* left-leaning national paper. Allegedly, a new Mining Authority would grant exploration and exploitation permits, instead of the Ministries of Economy and Environment. Industry representatives would dominate the Mining Authority, though it would incorporate some representation from government and ecological organizations. The Mining Authority would grant exploitation concessions automatically after a company receives an exploration license, whereas today an Environmental Impact Assessment and public consultation process are required. The proposed law allows one company to sell its property rights to another. According to the National Coalition on Metallic Mining, the PCN proposal would not regulate water usage or mandate compensation for damage, either.[18] Other sources confirmed most of these statements. In June 2007, Pacific Rim executives mentioned to me that they had suggested to President Saca's government to create a new regulatory agency that could be funded using the mining company's money. The PCN proposal would increase royalty rates from two percent to three percent, with the third percentage dedicated to funding the Mining Authority.

In the *Diario Co Latino*, the National Coalition on Metallic Mining claimed that Pacific Rim's lawyers drafted the PCN's proposal. One of those lawyers is the father of the vice president of Pacific Rim El Salvador, Rodrigo Chávez. Chávez, also an editorialist for the *El Diario de Hoy* newspaper, comes from a political family with connections to the elite business class. His father, Fidel Chávez Mena, was a presidential candidate in 1989 and 1994 for the Christian Democrat Party.

The National Coalition on Metallic Mining asserts that Pacific Rim has formed a relationship with Patricio Escobar Thompson, a representative of Grupo Poma, one of the most economically and politically powerful entities in El Salvador. Grupo Poma is a family-owned conglomerate of businesses, with most of its activities in El Salvador but some

# "You don't understand how things work here. There is the law in San Salvador and another law here. It does not matter what they say in the Assembly. There will be no mining here. We will not allow it."

that span across and outside of Central America: automobile dealerships, real estate development and construction, industrial manufacturing, hotels, telecommunications. Grupo Poma had over 10,000 employees in 2001. Patricio Escobar Thompson's wife, Ana Vilma de Escobar, is the Vice President of El Salvador.

Despite the potency of such putative political connections, whether or not the gold mining industry will develop is unclear. Most mining companies exited El Salvador by 2007. Pacific Rim was the last company to leave, in July 2008. By the end of the year, Pacific Rim had reduced its workforce and cut investments from about $1 million per month to $100,000.[19] "Pacific Rim was encouraged every step of the way by the highest levels of government," said Shrake, Pacific Rim's President and CEO, in explaining the company's decision to pull out of El Salvador. But "nothing has moved in the mining industry for two years." The company relocated its exploration work to Guatemala and Costa Rica, which has the same geological environment – a "fantastic, untapped gold belt" – but different political climate. According to Pacific Rim', the other Central American countries are more "politically stable for mining investment."[20]

On December 9, 2008, Pacific Rim issued a press release announcing that it had filed a Notice of Intent "to commence international arbitration proceeds" against El Salvador's government under the Central American Free Trade Agreement. The basis of Pacific Rim's claim was "the Government of El Salvador's breaches of international and El Salvadoran law arising out of the Government's failure, within its own

mandated time frames and pursuant to the clear terms of applicable laws, to issue exploration and exploitation permits to which the Company is entitled."[21] Pacific Rim plans to seek "compensation for the money [it] has spent in pursuit of its investments in El Salvador; damages for the loss of value that has been created by the Company through its efforts and investments resulting from the Government's wrongful conduct; costs associated with preparation for and conduct of the arbitration proceedings; and pre- and post- award interest on all claims." The arbitration process may take one to three years.

By CAFTA rules, Pacific Rim and the government of El Salvador had three months, until March 8, 2009, to "resolve their dispute amicably" before arbitration began. No such resolution occurred. Instead, on February 25, the new archbishop of El Salvador, Monseñor Luis Escobar Alas, spoke of the "grave damage" mining would bring in; the Director of the private National Foundation for Development (FUNDE), Roberto Rubio, endorsed the anti-mining movement.[22] Most significantly, President Saca made his first major public statement against mining, aired on a Catholic radio station. "No president, knowing the harm that [the industry] causes to public health, would dare to order his ministers to grant the permits. [Pacific Rim] is on the verge of opening an international claim, and I want to make one thing clear: I would prefer to pay $90 million than grant them a permit." Saca's statement was likely a political move in the run-up to the elections, with ARENA trailing the FMLN in the polls by as much as 15 percent, but the statement stands nonetheless.

## Conclusion

During interviews in Cabañas, I was taken aback by the lack of information and interest in mining among people whose lives and livelihoods would be the first ones affected if the gold mines opened. "I don't know, maybe mining is bad for water," one man said. "I went to a meeting. I heard from lots of people about water. But I don't know if it will affect the agriculture. I don't know much. I don't really want to be involved." Another interviewee said flatly, "I am not going to talk for or against mining. I do not like to fight. People who fight do not know what they are fighting for." "For me, I am outside the debate. I don't want to get involved. If they mine, okay. If they don't, then they don't." Other interviewees were not indifferent but resigned. "People say the company will take the gold and leave us poor," one interviewee said. "But I say take the gold or leave it, we will still be poor."

It is impossible to understand the current mining debate in El Salvador without considering its context: rural poverty and low education levels. Roughly 30 percent of the country's rural population was illiterate in 2002. In the department of Cabañas, youth go to school for only 3.7 years on average; the national average is 5.5 years.[23] The pressures of a subsistence lifestyle limit many people's critical analysis of this complicated issue or bring people to accept the industry for a lack of alternative options. "I oppose mining, but I accept the company's help," one interviewee said. "Who knows, maybe I will end up worse off later. But imagine! There is nobody here providing for us, and then comes Pacific Rim saying it will help us with our greatest needs."

The results of the CAFTA arbitration process and the new FMLN administration's position on mining are as yet unknown. Some analysts have questioned whether President-elect Funes will continue to oppose mining as obstinately as he did during his campaign once he is under pressure to govern and boost the rural economy. But the nature of the anti-mining movement is indisputably one of little compromise. During one interview in San Isidro with several leaders of the anti-mining movement, one of them squared his chair in front of mine and said, "Let me show you what negotiation means. Suppose you and I are the ones negotiating. I ask if you would rather give up your hand or your leg. What do you say? You see now. That is exactly how it is for us. We have nothing to negotiate with the mining company." When I asked about the possibility that the government might approve mining, another leader insisted, "You don't understand how things work here. There is the law in San Salvador and another law here. It does not matter what they say in the Assembly. There will be no mining here. We will not allow it."

These factors ought to play a significant role in national decision-making on mining: the context of rural poverty and low education rates; the probable distribution of potential environmental, economic, and social harms and benefits; the degree of neutrality and enforcement capacity of the government; the high levels of polarization and distrust; and the uncertainty inherent in the mining industry. These are the issues that ultimately determine who wins and who loses – and who can afford to lose – from gold mining in El Salvador.

Notes

[1] Keny Lopez Piche. "No a la mineria: Saca cierra puertas a explotacion de metales." La Prensa Grafica. 26 February 2009. <http://www.laprensagrafica.com/index.php/economia/nacional/32-nacional/20190-no-a-la-mineriasacacierra-puertas-a-explotacion-de-metales.html>

[2] Pacific Rim Mining Corp. <http://www.pacrim-mining.com/s/Home.asp>

[3] Programa de las Naciones Unidas para el Desarrollo (PNUD) Informe sobre Desarrollo Humano El Salvador 2003: Desafios y opciones en tiempos de globalizacion. Programa de las Naciones Unidas para el Desarrollo (PNUD). Primera edicion. San Salvador, El Salvador: PNUD, 2003.

[4] Pacific Rim Mining Corp. 2008 News Releases <http://www.pacrim-mining.com/s/News_2008.asp>

[5] "Gold, Oil Reach Highs Amid U.S. Recession Fears" 13 March 2008. CNN World Business. <http://www.cnn.com/2008/BUSINESS/03/13/world.markets/index.html>

[6] Ibid.

[7] Programa de las Naciones Unidas para el Desarrollo (PNUD) Informe sobre Desarrollo Humano El Salvador 2003: Desafios y opciones en tiempos de globalizacion. Programa de las Naciones Unidas para el Desarrollo (PNUD). Primera edicion. San Salvador, El Salvador: PNUD, 2003.

[8] Metodos Estudios y Procesos (MEP). Resultados Encuesta de Opiniones sobre el tema de la Explotacion Minera en El Salvador. January 2009.

[9] Instituto Universitario de Opinion Publica (IUDOP). Vicerrectoria de proyeccion social. Executive Summary: Knowledge and perceptions of mining in areas affected by mining activities in El Salvador. October 2007.

[10] Ibid.

[11] Thomas Power, "Metals Mining and Sustainable Development in Central America: An Assessment of Benefits and Costs." Oxfam America, 2008.

[12] Ibid.

[13] Goldcorp Inc., "San Martin," <www.goldcorp.com/operations/san_martin> (accessed 6 November 2007).

[14] Robert Moran. Mining Environmental Impacts: Integrating an Economic Perspective. 7 June 2000. Centro de Investigacion y Planificacion del Medio Ambiente. Santiago, Chile.

[15] Robert Moran. Technical Review of the El Dorado Mine Project Environmental Impact Assessment (EIA), El Salvador. October 2005.

[16] Manuel Enrique Hinds. Gold Mining in El Salvador: Costs and Benefits. June 2007.

[17] Thomas Power, "Metals Mining and Sustainable Development in Central America: An Assessment of Benefits and Costs." Oxfam America, 2008.

[18] Mineria Metalica: El Espelzunante Proyecto de Ley de Pacific Rim. 27 February 2008. <http://www.diariocolatino.com/es/20080227/opiniones/52548/>

[19] Ibid.

[20] Ibid.

[21] "Pacific Rim Files Notice of Intent to Seek CAFTA Arbitration. 9 December 2008. <http://www.pacrim-mining.com/s/News_2008.asp?ReportID=331320&_Type=2008-News-Releases&_Title=Pacific-Rim-Files-Notice-of-Intent-to-Seek-CAFTA-Arbitration>

[22] Keny Lopez Piche. "No a la mineria: Saca cierra puertas a explotacion de metales." La Prensa Grafica. 26 February 2009. <http://www.laprensagrafica.com/index.php/economia/nacional/32-nacional/20190-no-a-la-mineriasacacierra-puertas-a-explotacion-de-metales.html>

[23] Programa de las Naciones Unidas para el Desarrollo (PNUD) Informe sobre Desarrollo Humano El Salvador 2003.

# THE COMPLEX POWERLE

AN INSTITUTE
FOR GLOBAL LEADERSHIP
DR. JEAN MAYER GLOBAL
CITIZENSHIP LECTURE

SASKIA SASSEN

# ITY OF SSNESS

Saskia Sassen is the Robert S. Lynd Professor of Sociology at Columbia University. Her research and writing focuses on globalization (including social, economic and political dimensions), immigration, global cities (including cities and terrorism), the new networked technologies, and changes within the liberal state that result from current transnational conditions. In her research she has focused on the unexpected and the counterintuitive as a way to cut through established "truths." In her second book *The Global City*, she showed how the global economy, far from being placeless, has and needs very specific territorial insertions, and that this need is sharpest in the case of highly globalized and electronic sectors such as finance; this went against established notions at the time that the global economy transcended territory and its associated regulatory umbrellas. Her new books are *Territory, Authority, Rights: From Medieval to Global Assemblages* and *A Sociology of Globalization*. She recently completed for UNESCO a five-year project on sustainable human settlement, for which she set up a network of researchers and activists in over 30 countries. It is published as one of the volumes of the *Encyclopedia of Life Support Systems*.

Dr. Sassen received the Dr. Jean Mayer Global Citizenship Award as part of the 2009 Norris and Margery Bendetson EPIIC International Symposium on "Cities: Forging an Urban Future."

-

I'm not going to give you a neat, complete lecture. I really like incompleteness. And the city, in a way, really is about incompleteness. I'm really becoming a fan of incompleteness, because much of what is completed is actually rather problematic around the world.

Let me just start with setting a frame, a tone, an image. It is an invitation to think about global cities and global slums as emergent systemic actors, a very special kind of actor. They are an actor where powerlessness can become complex. It doesn't mean that you move to empowerment, but that the condition of being powerless becomes complex.

And here I want to just elaborate a bit on this notion of powerlessness. I've really been trying to understand in a way, do those without power also make history? They do, not always, but they do. But they do it under certain conditions. One of them is a temporal question. It takes more time for those without power to make history, than those with power. It can be generational; it can take three generations. So that is why the making of history does not necessarily empower. We really need to make that distinction.

Today, there are slums, global slums, which are quite different from the image that you have in English literature when the good and the kind wrote about the miseries of slums. There are such slums, too. But I'm referring to slums that really have emerged as political actors. Dharavi (Mumbai, India) is one such slum. The global city is a space where informal political actors can execute their project. By this, I mean actors who are not quite represented by traditional political organs like parties, political parties, labor unions, etc.

In this country, we tend to think, if you're going to do it and especially if it's about politics and you know those who don't have power, make sure that they get empowered. I think that's an admirable aim. But we have to open that up, because if we just stick with that, then all kinds of things become meaningless because people do not get empowered. Immigrants, asylum seekers, refugees, women who are persecuted – when they become subjects of human rights decisions, they often are not empowered. But by making the human rights regime work, they are actually strengthening the human rights regime even though they themselves do not become necessarily empowered. This is an example of the complexity of powerlessness.

The question then becomes under what conditions, in what spaces, vis a vis what kinds of struggles, do those without power become able to transform that powerlessness into a complex condition of powerlessness? And here is where the city and this emergent, systemic of the global slum, enter into the picture. The global city is one of those spaces.

Let me give you another example, just to illustrate. You may recall that two years ago, the American Congress was debating criminalizing illegal immigration. Right now, you are in violation of the law when you are in the US illegally or without documentation, but it's not a criminal act. So the criminalization would have been a very serious escalation of the condition of being in violation of residence laws. Massive demonstrations occurred in response to the debate, half a million people in Chicago, half a million in Los Angeles, half a million in New York. There were people with signs, "I have the right to have rights." And no one checked to see if they were illegal. In the space of the city, an individual becomes easily part of a multitude, especially if there is a political project.

But how does space change that? Imagine that same immigrant who was holding a sign on the streets of Los Angeles, holding that sign on a farm in California, "I have the right to have rights." His employer would have come and said, "Come on, go back to work," or worse, would have called the INS [Immigration and Naturalization Service] and had him arrested, but not in the city.

So were these immigrants who demonstrated, including the undocumented, empowered? Not necessarily, but their powerlessness became complex.

The question of these demonstrations, of contested political actions, in the space of the city, is an illustration of how the space of the global city contains the capacity to transform powerlessness, not into empowerment, but into a complex condition. And in being complex, it contains the possibility of politics.

Now I am sure that many of you know of examples of small organizations that struggled for years to achieve their goals. It may have looked like it was an impossible task, yet many of these succeeded. Remember the woman [Wangari Maathai] who won the Nobel Prize, who planted trees with a bunch of other women in Kenya? Those are initiatives that seem very partial, very micro, that seem they're going to go nowhere, but they build up. Do they actually empower the people who plant those trees? You can't quite say that, strictly speaking. But something is changed, and something is changed because something is made.

Now, the space of the global slum, and here Dharavi's probably the most famous slum. The space of the global slum is a space that begins to have that quality. It's not all slums that have this capacity to emerge as the global slum and, in fact, alter the meaning of slum. Some slums are truly spaces of pure misery, destitution that is absolute. There, the powerlessness of the people is absolutely elementary. Nothing happens. That is not quite the global slum. It's not, as I was saying before, the meaning that you would have, you know, in the typical sociology text of twenty years ago, where the slum is almost a word that you don't use because it signals a racializing of space. That has changed, but only in a political context.

Now the slum is also a political systemic actor. Dharavi is a very good example, but so are the favelas in Sao Paulo where Lula's [Luiz Inácio Lula da Silva, the current President of Brazil] Labor Party made sure that everybody was registered to vote. Four million people voted in those favelas in Sao Paulo, and they voted for Lula. So, they are still slum dwellers. They still have all the discomforts, all the disadvantages, all the shortcomings. But they are also making history.

I talked about powerlessness; now let me move to power. I like to think about power as something that is made. Power is not just a condition. It's not just an attribute that you have or you don't have. And, again, I think of the space of the global city as being space that also makes power. It's also a space that has the conditions to make capital, including the making of this kind of financial capital that we are living with now.

Earlier, when I referred to informal political actors, I was also thinking about the multinational corporation, because the multinational corporation is a private economic persona, not a political persona. But at a period of transformation, such as the last twenty years, the global city becomes one of the spaces where such corporate actors can make politics, make the political, beyond the question of lobbies and all of that, in reshaping the space of the city so it becomes a platform for their operations.

This notion of the actual space of cities, and what I'm thinking about is the dense aggregation of a whole variety of activities for economic reasons, is a critical part of the making of power in the global city. These are centers for the production of management functions, of coordination functions. It is really the capacity to manage global operations. It's also a frontier space.

For instance, if you think of finance, finance is an invasive practice. It is not like traditional banking. Traditional banking, you have the money, and you sell it for a high rate of interest or for a low one. Finance is about the money that you don't have, whether that starts at ten billion or at a hundred. So finance is invasive, which means that it always is entering a space that is not its own and it's going to acquire that space; it's going to control it, it's going to use it. For finance to grow, it needs to invade other sectors. So, it

financializes our debt, our credit card debts, etc. It financializes all kinds of things. Now, that means that the financial center, and as global finance grew there were more and more financial centers in global cities, is a very particular space. It's a space where the actually quite standardized, though very complex, global financial system encounters the thick and local practices, of a national or local economy. The financial center, the global city, is this space for a set of very particular cultural operations, which is to persuade the local financial elites, the local economic elites, the local investors to accept the desirability of whatever the instruments are that are getting sold.

So, the financial center is actually a very particular space where a very thick local culture with informal systems of trust, etc, confronts this more standardized, transnational global financial actor. And one image that I like to use when I think of frontier space is that the global city is a frontier space, which means that two actors from different worlds encounter each other, but there are no rules for engagement for those two actors.

The global GDP in the whole world is $54 trillion. The total amount of derivatives – that is the ultimate instrument for finance to get from what you have to what you don't have – is $650 trillion. What really brought the current system down were credit default swaps. Credit default swaps were $1 trillion in 2001, and $62 trillion in 2008. In seven years, they grew 62 times. There are very few things that grow that fast. That is finance.

Now here's the irony: the irony is, the global city and the financial center – this networked system – they were good at financializing, at inventing – instruments had to be invented to produce these outcomes.

They made it so well that more and more sectors of the economy were financialized. Now we have a crisis. And one way of describing the crisis is that finance cannot find enough sectors – enough things that are outside its frame – that have not been financialized to make up for the $160 trillion right now in debt, three times global GDP. That is an incredible contradiction. And the global city is a space that knew how to produce that outcome.

Let me talk a little about the subprime mortgage, because it is important. Made in America, the intention was supposedly to provide housing for modest income people. But it became financialized and became another version of powerlessness becoming complex but not necessarily empowering.

So financing invented a conduit mechanism, a link that made it possible to achieve the following condition. The condition was that you could actually use millions of mortgages of modest income people where, there was really not a lot of money involved and mix them up with other instruments, because investors wanted asset-backed investments. So, you could say there is a mortgage in here, though it was split into a thousand little items. And then the financial system created a separate instrument so that whether the person who had the mortgage could or could not pay that mortgage was absolutely irrelevant to the profit for the investor. That's magic. Clearly they over did it, and they fell flat on their faces. Because now a lot of very powerful investors have been brought down by millions of these very small mortgages. It is estimated in the next four years, ten to 12 million people will lose their homes to foreclosure. This is an incredibly destructive mechanism, but at the same time, I want to recover a systemic condition in this, which is that these modest income people, who were subjected to a kind of primitive accumulation, actually as it is scaled up and as a collectivity, brought down some very powerful investors. Now that is another thing that these very complex spaces make possible.

This is the condition of being powerless that scales that position up to a systemic mechanism that actually has a much broader impact. But empowerment does not necessarily come about.

Now, ideally we all want empowerment and I do like this pragmatism in the American culture. You want results; you want good results; you want positive results. They don't always come. I was just at a conference this morning on the world social forums [Ponte Allegre]. And what have they achieved? So have they empowered a lot of people, but have they empowered the landless? Not really. A lot of the work that needs to be done, the politics work, whether in cities or slums or some other space, does not necessarily produce empowerment. And there is the risk that we stand back and we say that this is not worth doing. What I'm trying to argue is that in many, often ironic ways, rendering powerlessness complex is a kind of interesting mechanism in the making of a larger political project. Even if empowerment doesn't directly follow, it might eventually follow.

I mean, in our country, the civil rights struggles went on for generations, before one good day in 1964, Congress woke up and said let's give them some rights. Behind that decision were generations of struggle. It's a way really of repositioning all kinds of struggles and efforts, which are parts of eventual possibilities and successes.

I wrote a little article about the next US President, it just came out now in February in *Dissent*. I said the next President is going to have more power than any President before him. And I ended that piece in slightly an ironic tone. Perhaps the executive, with all this power, could actually use that excess of power to democratize the country. And the point here is that there is work to be done.

The city is the space where – when we address global governance challenges, whether the challenges are about the environment, race, or religious intolerance – they become concrete. In cities, they become urgent. So the city really emerges as one of these grand strategic spaces for all kinds of actions.

/ END

# AMERICA
# NIGHTMA
# UNDERST
# THE MOR
# CRISIS

# N RE ANDING GAGE

JESSICA HERRMANN

Jessica Herrmann is a senior economics major at Tufts University. Jessica conducted independent research in Israel on the inequality in the Israeli health care system as a member of the 2007-2008 EPIIC class on "Global Poverty and Inequality". She spent the summer of 2008 working at Boston Community Capital, which sparked her interest in the foreclosure crisis and its impact on Boston communities. Jessica has expanded her initial research at Boston Community Capital into a senior honors thesis on the topic of foreclosures in the Boston area. Her thesis research explores the maintenance of properties post-foreclosure by banks and examines the differences in the spatial clustering in the current foreclosure crisis to that of the foreclosure crisis in the early 1990s in Boston. Jessica was the recipient of both the Charles G. Bluhdorn Prize in Economics and the Lewis F. Manly Memorial Prize and received highest honors for her thesis.

On July 23, 2008, Carlene Balderrama, a 52-year-old woman from Taunton, Massachusetts, started her day like any other. She watched her husband and her 24-year-old son leave the house, ran her errands and cleaned the house. But then she went to the kitchen table and wrote out two notes, she faxed the first one and left the second on the table. She then walked into the living room and put the barrel of her husband's high-powered rifle into her mouth and ended her life. The first letter was sent to her mortgage company, which had scheduled a foreclosure on her home at five o-clock that evening, 90 minutes after her suicide. Balderrama had failed to make her mortgage payments for 42 months. Her fax stated that she would be dead before they came to foreclose on her home.

Despite the family's significant financial problems Carlene's husband was completely in the dark. Carlene had been in charge of the family's bills and had shredded the letters from the mortgage company before her husband could find them. Her husband returned home to find his wife dead and her suicide note on the kitchen table, which told him to use her life insurance to pay off their debt. Deepening the already incomprehensible family suffering, Carlene's last selfless attempt to save her family from financial ruin was in vain as suicide is not covered under life insurance policies. Though Balderrama's story seems inconceivable, stories like hers are likely to become more prevalent as the pressures of the mortgage crisis weigh down on individuals facing foreclosure.

### Understanding Mortgages

It is impossible to begin to discuss the mortgage crisis without first understanding mortgages and their importance. A mortgage is "a loan to finance the purchase of real estate, usually with specified payment periods and interest rates."[1] A payment period is the amount of time the mortgagee has to repay the loan, typically either 15 or 30 years, though longer and shorter terms are possible. There are two main types of mortgages, fixed rate and adjustable rate. A fixed rate mortgage (FRM) has a set interest rate for the entire period of the loan, while an adjustable rate mortgage (ARM) has a rate that can change throughout the payment period. The most common ARM, accounting for two-thirds of all recent ARMs[2], is called a "2/28," where the interest rate is a set "teaser" rate for the first two years of the mortgage and then increases to a higher adjustable rate for the last 28 years[3]. Adjustable rate mortgages usually have an interest rate based on a base index (the adjustable rate), which is then added to a fixed number, known as the spread. The most common base index for ARMs is the London Interbank Offered Rate (LIBOR), which typically has a value of between five and seven percent.

Mortgages are typically used as a means to provide the necessary collateral to afford the purchase of a home. Homeownership is typically the largest investment of an individual's life. In a 2006 report by the Center for Responsible Lending, the authors wrote, "for most families, homeownership is the most accessible path to economic security and is associated with a host of non-economic benefits, including safer neighborhoods, better health and higher educational attainment."[4] Because the value of a home is expected to appreciate over an extended period of time, owning a home can be seen as a long-term investment. In addition, there is a sense of pride and accomplishment for individuals who achieve homeownership, often seen as a pillar of the "American Dream."

## Subprime Loans

The subprime mortgage market, which is currently viewed as the major culprit in today's financial crisis, was originally meant to be a means of increasing access to mortgages for individuals who would not have been approved in the prime market. Mortgages in the prime market are provided to individuals with high credit scores who pose little risk of defaulting on their loans. The subprime market "is intended to provide home loans for people with impaired or limited credit histories."[5] The borrowers in the subprime market would not qualify for prime loans as a result of their high loan-to-value ratios, high debt-to-income ratios, low documentation and low credit scores[6]. The loan-to-value ratio is the ratio between the amount of the loan and the value of the property; the debt-to-income ratio is just that, the ratio between the amount of debt that the mortgage causes and the individual's income. Low documentation refers to little or no documentation of the individual's income, which is overlooked in the subprime market. All of these factors make it impossible for the individual to receive a mortgage from the prime market.

The subprime market came about as a result of the Depository Institutions Deregulation and Monetary Control Act in 1980, which permitted interest rate caps, and the Mortgage Transaction Parity Act of 1982, which allowed variable interest rates and balloon payments[7]. These two acts essentially made subprime lending legal and allowed the lenders to place

# THOSE SUBPRIME MORTGAGES THAT DO RESULT IN HOME PURCHASES ARE FOUND TO BE SIX TIMES MORE LIKELY TO END IN FORECLOSURE THAN PURCHASE MORTGAGES IN THE PRIME MARKET.

the increased presence of subprime loans in the mortgage market, the impact of low performance in the subprime market has a large impact on the overall market.

The current mortgage crisis has revolved around the phrase "subprime mortgage" as a result of the high foreclosure rate among subprime mortgages. The statistics on the foreclosure rate in the subprime market in recent years can be defined at best as frightening. Those subprime mortgages that do result in home purchases are found to be six times more likely to end in foreclosure than purchase mortgages in the prime market[10]. This is a result of the riskier types of borrowers and the higher interest rates and fees that are associated with subprime loans. In addition, "as many as one in eight subprime loans originated between 1998 and 2004 ended in foreclosure within five years."[11] These numbers are staggering, and the sudden influx of foreclosures was not just a fluke in the system, but a confluence of a number of different problems.

higher interest rates and fees on higher-risk borrowers. In addition to these laws, the increase in the subprime market was in large part a result of changes in the market interest rates. "In 1994, for example, interest rates increased and the volume of originations in the prime market dropped." As a result, the subprime market grew in size to balance the decline in the prime market. This market has quickly grown; in 1998 the share of mortgages originating in the subprime market was only ten percent, whereas in 2006 it was 23 percent[8]. However, it has been estimated that since 1998, "only nine percent of subprime loans have gone to first-time homebuyers."[9]

This means that the majority of subprime loans are refinances. Refinancing is a process by which an individual will pay off an existing mortgage by taking out a new mortgage. This new mortgage can be for a higher value, have a different payment period and/or have a different interest rate. The importance of refinancing will be discussed in further depth later, but it is important to realize that even with the higher percentage of subprime mortgages, the majority of them do not result in new homeownership. Because of

## : Why Now? Causes and Beneficiaries of the Current Crisis

### Predators

One of the main explanations that can be seen in the media today is that predatory lending was taking place. A predatory mortgage loan is defined as "an unsuitable loan designed to exploit vulnerable and unsophisticated borrowers."[12] These loans tend to contain at least one of the following characteristics: higher interest rates and fees than necessary, "abusive terms and conditions that trap borrowers and lead to a spiral of increased indebtedness", and the targeting of women, the elderly and minorities (especially those who have equity in their homes)[13]. Subprime loans are already riskier because of the prevalence of adjustable interest rates, balloon payments (bulk payments made at the end of the payment period to pay off the remaining value of the loan), prepayment penalties (lenders charge fees to borrowers if they pay their mortgages off early), and little or no documentation used when writing the loan[14]. The risk caused by subprime loans is increased dramatically when predatory lending takes place. The major culprit in predatory lending is the mortgage broker. According to the US Department of Housing and Urban Development, "mortgage brokers are involved in about 60 percent of all mortgage loan transactions."[15]

When an individual takes out a mortgage, he can either work directly with the mortgager or through a mortgage broker, who works as a link between the borrower and the lender. "Mortgage brokers, who originate the majority of subprime mortgages, have a strong incentive to close as many loans as possible, but very little reason to consider the loans' future performance."[16] Because mortgage brokers are writing the loans, but do not pay the costs of a default, they are less likely to concern themselves with borrowers' ability to repay the loan. Not only is the mortgage broker not held accountable for a default on the loan, but there are even incentives for mortgage brokers to create loans with higher interest rates and write a large number of loans, without consideration for the quality of the loan. An example of this is that some brokers "collect a 'yield-spread premium,' which is a cash bonus a broker receives for charging a higher interest rate on a loan than the lender required."[17] This leaves many wondering how it is possible that mortgage brokers could be writing loans that were impossible for the borrower to pay. The main explanation is that there is a lack of regulation and legal consequences for "making home loans that are predictably unsustainable."[18] With incentives to produce high interest loans and little or no care for the loan's performance, mortgage brokers were a major cause of the high rate of default on subprime mortgages.

The mortgage brokers put the borrower in contact with the lender, typically a bank. Within the subprime mortgage crisis there have been a number of banks that have been major players. The top ten subprime lenders in Massachusetts between 1993 and 2007 (according to research conducted by Christopher Foote using the Warren Group dataset and the list of subprime lenders provided by the Department of Housing and Urban Development) included Option One Mortgage Corporation, Fremont Investment & Loan, Long Beach Mortgage Company and First Franklin Financial[19]. The top ten lenders accounted for 41,114 sub-

prime loans that were issued in this 14-year period, 68.1 percent of which were subprime purchase mortgages[20]. The top subprime lender in Massachusetts during this period was Option One Mortgage Corporation, which issued 11,243 subprime loans[21]. All ten of these lenders have since been shutdown[22].

So how did these banks and mortgage brokers get away with their predatory lending practices? The fault lies in the lack of regulation of the mortgage sector, an issue that is not easily fixed. Because high interest rates and additional fees are common in high-risk loans, it is difficult to distinguish predatory loans from loans that were highly risky and therefore required a higher expense on the part of the borrower. In some cases, these high interest loans are necessary for the borrower to be able to receive a loan at all, due to the risk to the lender. According to a 2001 publication by Fannie Mae, additional complications arise in regulating subprime loans because "there is little, if any, publicly available data regarding loan terms, such as interest rates, origination points, processing or closing fees, and special provisions such as balloon payments, credit life insurance, and prepayment restrictions."[23] This makes it difficult to investigate the origination of the loan and its costs to the borrower in order to categorize it as a subprime or predatory loan. The article continues by explaining that even with "a clear technical distinction between legitimate subprime lending and predatory lending, there exists a huge gray area between the two,"[24] making it difficult to place firm regulations on high risk lending that would protect borrowers from predatory lenders. Regulating high risk lending could potentially eliminate subprime lending entirely, putting the government in a difficult situation.

## Why Foreclosures Are Increasing

There are additional trends that have been present with subprime borrowers that have increased the rate of foreclosure. One of these trends has been a decline in the amount of money put into the home, the down payment. In the prime market, if the borrower is not able to put down at least 20 percent of the value of the home, he is required to pay for private mortgage insurance (PMI), which will cover the lender's losses if the loan cannot be repaid or the value of the mortgage is not recovered in foreclosure and subsequent sale.

Many subprime purchases are made with little to no equity in the homes, meaning that the homeowner has a low level of investment in their home. Typically the buyer takes out more than one purchase mortgage and the cumulative value of the mortgages is the purchase price of the home. "In 2007, 40 percent of Massachusetts residents who lost their homes to foreclosure had put no money down when they bought their homes"[25] and "52.4 percent [of these Massachusetts residents] put down less than five percent."[26]

In addition to a lack of equity in their homes, there has been a high level of refinancing of mortgages. As already noted, refinancing takes place to change the payment period, interest rate, value and terms of a loan. Refinancing has been used in recent years as a method to remove equity from the home by taking out higher valued mortgages. "American households have used refinances...to pull money out of their homes at an unprecedented rate: over two trillion dollars in the past five years alone."[27] The declining equity in the homes has the same affect as not having a down payment, there is a smaller investment being made by the homeowner. An increase in the number of refinances has a direct impact on the likelihood of foreclosure. "Homes that were purchased in 1999 and foreclosed upon in 2007 had an average of 1.6 subprime mortgages during their ownership experiences. The comparable number for homes purchased in 1999 that have not yet been foreclosed upon or sold is only 0.2."[28] Furthermore, the risk of losing one's home increases by 36 percent for borrowers that refinance more than once[29]. One of the main reasons for the increase in refinancing and loss of equity in the homes is the downward turn in the economy.

### The Financial Crisis

Increasing food costs and high unemployment rates are just a few of the signs of our declining economy, which has had an important effect on increasing foreclosures. "Over the past two decades, after-tax income for the bottom 60 percent of families climbed only five to 15 percent, while costs for such basics as housing, child care, and health care rose 53 to 75 percent."[30] An increasing cost of living has resulted in an inability for many borrowers to keep up with their mortgage payments. In addition to the higher costs, there is more uncertainty of one's income: "a 2004 study reported that the average annual variation in income for middle-income households... has doubled since the 1970s,"[31] making large mortgage payments harder to payoff. Overall, these factors combine to create an atmosphere where individuals have less flexibility in terms of their income. A major addition to this problem is that in recent years there has been a significant decline in the savings rate of individuals. The personal savings rate has declined over the past two decades and has actually been negative since midway through the year 2005[32]. This is not unique to the US. In fact, there has been a decline in the savings rate across the majority of the 30 Organization for Economic Co-Operation and Development countries since the beginning of the 1990s[33]. Specifically, the savings rate in the United States declined by 3.0 percent between 1995 and 2000[34]. During this same period, the savings rate in Italy declined by 7.3, the savings rate in Canada declined by 3.9 percent, and the savings rate in the United Kingdom declined by 4.4 percent[35].

A lack of savings means that borrowers are unable to deal with shocks to their income or large increases in their mortgage payments. We have already discussed the prevalence of ARMs in the subprime market. Because the rates are constantly changing, these mortgages provide more uncertainty to the borrower. The increase in interest rates over recent years has resulted in unexpected additions to the monthly payments on ARM mortgages. A low savings rate means that many borrowers were unable to afford the change and were forced into foreclosure. In addition to the increase in interest rates over recent years, the down turning economy has also brought higher unemployment rates; job loss for individuals with little to no savings makes it impossible to keep up with mortgage payments. Because these individuals have little or no money to draw from when they lose their jobs or face unexpected costs, they are "likely to attach a steep discount to future payoffs" on their home from the appreciation rate; they are in need of cash and so are willing to forego future benefits from homeownership in return for money now[36]. These people are likely to go into foreclosure or try to sell their homes as a means of increasing their current wellbeing, but they lose the possibility of wealth accumulation that comes from homeownership[37].

A complicating factor is declining house prices. This decline has had an important impact on the number of foreclosures in recent years. A decline in house prices means that typical methods for borrowers to get out of mortgage trouble, such as refinancing their mortgages, taking out home loans, or selling are now out of the picture[38]. Once prices decline, many homeowners can no longer sell their homes for a price that is high enough to pay off their mortgages because mortgages are taken out based on the original purchase price. Declining housing prices cause a situation of negative equity in the home, where the value of the loans taken out on the home is actually greater than the house's worth. The decline in house prices has a direct effect on the foreclosure rate. "A borrower who has seen his property's value fall by more than 20 percent since the initial purchase is 15 times more likely to lose the home to foreclosure relative to someone who has seen his property appreciate by 20 percent"[39]. It is important to note that although foreclosure rates are higher during periods of low or no housing appreciation, this does not mean that there are not failed loans during times of high appreciation[40]. The difference is that during times of high appreciation, it is possible for homeowners to avoid foreclosure through refinancing their loans or selling their property, whereas with low or declining appreciation rates, this is not an option. Because borrowers in the subprime market are constantly on the edge of defaulting, they are incredibly sensitive to changes in the appreciation rate of their homes[41].

### The Bundlers

There were foreclosure filings for one in every 534 American homes in January of 2008, yet there is still no solution[42]. One of the most significant complications in the current mortgage market is the secondary market. In order to decrease the risk of loss due to loan default, lenders sell their loans to investors; this creates a "secondary market" for mortgage loans[43]. The origination of this process was in the 1970s when the first mortgage-backed securities were sold to investors. These initial loans were sold to investors as individual loans[44]. This process has changed through the years, and now the mortgages are bundled together by investors to be resold as securities; these securities include both high and low risk mortgages. The first of these collateralized debt obligations (CDOs) was created by Michael Milken in 1987[45], and this unregulated market of reselling mortgages has grown in size since its start. It is attractive to both investors and lenders because "investors now [have] a liquid instrument and lenders [have] the option to move any interest rate risk associated with mortgages off of their balance sheet.[46]" According to Cameron L. Cowan, speaking on behalf of the American Securitization Forum, the benefits of securitization are numerous. He explains that "chief among these [benefits] is the contribution of securitization to lower borrowing costs both for individuals and corporations."[47] He continues by noting the increased flexibility provided to the loan originators and the additional opportunities for investment.[48]

The securities are rated to indicate how risky they are, although it is almost impossible to find out the exact contents and "CDO ratings may mislead investors because they can obscure the risk of default."[49] Although ratings are not necessarily accurate, the securities deemed as "riskier" are given lower preference in being paid off. This means that if a borrower defaults on a loan, the investors with the least risky loans receive payment first; they are followed by the next lowest risk investors, and those with the riskiest securities are paid off last, if at all. Because mortgages are packaged into securities and then sold off, it is nearly impossible to determine the 'true owner' of specific mortgages and the investors are "protected by a legal doctrine called 'holder in due course' which prevents borrowers from making claims against the purchaser of their loan, even if, for example, that loan contained abusive features."[50] This causes significant problems for borrowers who begin to face default on loans that they should not have been given in the first place. These borrowers have no way to combat the faulty loans they were given and are forced to either face foreclosure or find a way to keep up with unsustainable mortgage payments. "As of June 30, 2006, mortgage-backed securities were the largest segment of the United States bond market, accounting for 23 percent of all bond market debt outstanding."[51] The impact of increasing foreclosures has had a direct impact on investors who purchased the securities and is one of the many negative results of the mortgage crisis.

## Are there victims?

Many subprime lenders lacked the financial saviness necessary to understand the role a mortgage is meant to play and the types of mortgages best suited for their needs. In focus groups conducted by Boston Community Capital in July 2008 with homeowners in Boston who were facing foreclosure, many explained that they were in this situation today as a result of being told that they could essentially use their homes as ATMs, removing equity when they needed money. There was no consideration for the fact that appreciation rates could fall and that this could result in the loss of their homes.

Because borrowers saw their homes as a source of income, not an investment for the future, they continuously removed equity from their homes, which resulted in higher mortgage payments. Many of the borrowers were "on the edge," meaning that they could pay their mortgage payments each month, but just barely. As a result, if there was any unexpected expense or decline in income, the individuals could no longer pay off their debt. Unfortunately, Merrill Lynch has predicated that housing prices are unlikely to increase in coming years. They have forecasted a decline in housing prices by 15 percent in 2008, ten percent in 2009 and five percent in 2010[52]. This means it is unlikely that the situation will improve in the next few years.

Within the focus groups conducted by Boston Community Capital, a number of the participants explained their troubles as a result of "bad luck". This included job loss, illness, divorce and death. As a result of these situations, the borrowers could no longer afford their payments and ended up in foreclosure. This is closely linked to the decline in the savings rate, which was discussed earlier. Without a financial cushion for times of trouble, any change in the borrower's income resulted in a default on their loans. The fault for this can be found in both the borrower and the lender. The borrowers lacked the necessary preparation for dealing with a fluctuation in their income, while the lenders were providing loans with monthly payments that the borrowers could just barely afford.

In order to gain a better understanding of the "normal" scenario, I will walk us through a common borrower's situation. Although there is truly no single case that could be used to represent the experiences of all borrowers, this scenario is based on my own research of the mortgage history of over 900 borrowers who went into foreclosure during the period between December 2007 and June 2008. Let's start with our borrower, Fred. Fred purchased his home in 2003 for $200,000. He received a first purchase mortgage for $150,000 and a second mortgage for $50,000, both from the same lender. The first purchase mortgage was a 30-year adjustable rate mortgage with an initial rate of six percent and an adjusted rate of LIBOR plus 5.75 percent. His second purchase mortgage was a 15-year, fixed rate mortgage with an interest rate of eight percent. You will notice that this means that Fred has now purchased a new home without paying a penny out of pocket. After two years, Fred decides to refinance both of his mortgages. The first purchase mortgage is refinanced as a 30-year adjustable rate mortgage, but this time the interest rates are slightly higher than his original interest rates, and the second purchase mortgage is refinanced and becomes a $75,000 mortgage with a similar fixed interest rate. In 2006, Fred begins to experience higher expenses, maybe his child gets sick or he loses his job, and he can no longer pay off his larger mortgage. The larger mortgage then goes into foreclosure and because Fred now has negative equity in the home and housing prices have declined since his original purchase, he cannot sell the home for enough money that he can pay off his debt. Sadly, Fred loses his home and must find a new place to buy or rent.

## Shock Waves : Cyclical Consequences

The impact of a foreclosure spreads from the investor, who purchased a share of mortgage, to the city where the foreclosure takes place. Let's start by looking at the most obvious effect, that of the foreclosure on the individual. There are

"As of June 30, 2006, mortgage-backed securities were the largest segment of the United States bond market, accounting for 23 percent of all bond market debt outstanding."

the obvious emotional impacts of foreclosure, the most extreme being the example of Carlene Balderrama. Foreclosure results in a decrease in an individual's credit score, which makes it more difficult for an individual to acquire loans in the future and, when one can receive a loan, the payment will be much higher[53]. Additionally, as already discussed, homeownership is an opportunity for wealth accumulation over the long term. The loss of one's home means the loss of opportunity for future capital gain. It has been estimated by the Center for Responsible Lending that "subprime loans made during 1998-2006 have led or will lead to a net loss of homeownership for almost one million families;"[54] that is one million families who have lost the chance to accumulate long-term wealth. They have estimated that almost 15.6 percent of the subprime loans that have been written since 1998 either have or will end in foreclosure [55]. Not only does the increase in foreclosure mean that the borrower loses the possible wealth accumulation from the current property, but "research indicates that homeowners who give up homeownership for any reason can take more than a decade to get back in"[56]. The loss of the "American Dream" and one of the greatest opportunities for wealth accumulation can be impossible to reclaim.

The increase in foreclosures has a significant impact on both the cities and neighborhoods being hit hardest. The cities lose the tax revenue that comes from occupied homes[57]; the Homeownership Preservation Fund has done a study on the impact of foreclosure on the cities and has estimated that the "typical cost incurred by the city for a vacant foreclosed property sold at auction [is] between $5,400 and $7,000."[58] When there are five or even ten foreclosure auctions on a single street, the costs to a city are anything but insignificant. Because there tends to be a high concentration of foreclosures in specific neighborhoods, the impact on communities is debilitating. The results of vacant, boarded-up and abandoned houses range from a further divestment in the community to lower levels of social capital. Abandoned buildings provide locations for the selling and use of drugs, foster increased criminal activity, and can become the home for neighborhood trash, squatters and stray animals [59]. In addition, abandoned buildings become a source of income for criminals who will raid the properties and remove copper wiring and other building components that can be resold for profit[60].

In looking at the effects of foreclosures on crime, Dan Immergluck, an Associate Professor in the City and Regional Program in the College of Architecture at Georgia Institute of Technology, and Geoff Smith, a Research Project Director at the Woodstock Institute, found a causal relationship. In their study, they discovered that "an increase of... about 2.8 foreclosures for every 100 owner-occupied properties in one year... corresponds to an increase in neighborhood violent crime of approximately 6.7 percent."[61] An increase in violence, drugs, and overall criminal activity has a direct impact on the desirability of the community.

Immergluck and Smith did another study on the impact of foreclosures on housing prices. They concluded that "each conventional foreclosure within an eighth of a mile of a single-family home results in a 0.9 percent decline in the value of that home"[62] and that "properties located within 150 feet of an abandoned unit sold for over $7,000 less than other properties."[63] As we have already discussed, the decline in housing prices has had a major impact on the increase in foreclosures. Because of the direct link between foreclosures in a neighborhood on the property values of surrounding homes, foreclosures tend to be highly concentrated in certain areas. This concentration tends to be in poorer, minority areas. This is a result of the fact that the lower-income homeowners are unable to acquire mortgages from the prime market and that over half of all loans to African American borrowers are subprime loans, while four-tenths of loans to Latinos are subprime loans[64].

There has also been a significant impact on the creditors. Listening to the news, it is impossible to avoid hearing about the number of lenders and investors who have gone bankrupt as a result of the mortgage crisis. On one website dedicated to keeping track of these "imploded lenders," there are 277 creditors listed as those that have "imploded" since late 2006 and 19 listed as "ailing" lenders[65]. Included under the list of "imploded lender" are the well-known cases of Bear Stearns and Wells Fargo and the less notorious names of National Wholesale Funding and KH Financial[66]. The impact of foreclosures is both significant and widespread, but what can be done to stop it?

## Salvation?

Currently the United States Government has enacted a plan to provide nearly four billion dollars in funding to assist areas that were hit the hardest by the mortgage crisis. "Congress mandated that the money [provided] be allocated based on the number and percentage of foreclosures, homes financed with subprime loans, and homes in default or delinquency in the community. Once the formula is set, [the United States Department of Housing and Development] has 30 days to dole out the funds. Government officials then have 18 months to put the money to use in their neighborhoods."[67] The goal is to increase the availability of affordable housing while simultaneously decreasing the number of vacant properties. "Sean O'Toole, founder of foreclosureradar.com, a foreclosed properties website for real estate professionals... [declared that] '$4 billion is kind of a meaningless sum... It can't possibly make a difference. You've brought a pistol to a nuclear war.'"[68] Considering the extent of the problem and the cost to renovate many of these homes, this response is understandable.

Another attempt being made to seek retributions for the cost of the mortgage crisis is through the law. There have been 170 cases "filed in federal courts during the first three months of 2008"[69]. With these additional cases, it is highly probable that the "subprime mortgage and related filings – now totaling 448 cases over the 15 months ending March 31, 2008 – will soon surpass the 559 savings-and-loan cases of the early 1990s."[70] However, because the majority of these cases have not been closed, it is impossible to know the impact they will play in the current crisis and it is unlikely that they will provide the compensation needed by the extensive number of families who have lost their homes. Given that these current efforts are inadequate to meet the needs of the nation, it is necessary to look at what else can be done.

The major emphasis of efforts to deal with the current crisis should be on preventing future foreclosures. This begins with increasing regulation in the origination process of the mortgages and decreasing the incentives for mortgage brokers to create unsustainable loans. An important alteration to the process, which has been advocated by the Center for Responsible Lending, would be to create set pricing for subprime markets that is transparent and has "market-driven prices for mortgages representing similar risks"[71]. This change would decrease the opportunities for predatory lending and unfair pricing for less knowledgeable borrowers. Lenders should be required to create sustainable loans, which take into account the loan-to-value ratio, debt-to-income ratio and the borrower's unique situation. The borrower should be able to repay the loan even if housing prices decline or interest rates increase. There is currently no room for adjustment. "Almost half of Massachusetts forecloses had owned their homes for less than three years."[72] Because the foreclosure process itself takes approximately six months, this means that borrowers were facing default on their loans less than two and a half years after receiving their loans, an exceptionally short period of time. Lenders must not allow their borrowers to purchase their homes without equity, as this is a lower investment by the owner and is less likely to be successful.

This is a result of the fact that the lower-income homeowners are unable to acquire mortgages from the prime market and that over half of all loans to African American borrowers are subprime loans, while four-tenths of loans to Latinos are subprime loans.

Additionally, Alan Mallach at the Metropolitan Policy Program at the Brookings Institution explains that one of the steps that state governments should take is to both ensure a fair foreclosure process (one that provides the owner with adequate time to attempt to sell his/her home, provides clear notices to the borrower of the impending foreclosure, etc.) and encourage lenders to pursue alternative options to foreclosure[73]. Lenders must be willing to be flexible and to adjust the rates and payment periods for loans that are currently in default. Readjusting the mortgage payments so that they are sustainable can salvage some of these mortgages. Banks face higher costs in foreclosure and holding the properties than they will from refinancing the loans.

Unfortunately, there is no easy solution to the mortgage crisis, and it does not appear to be ending in the near future. In fact, it has turned much worse. With the fall of Fannie Mae and Freddie Mac, the selling of Lehman Brothers, and the billions of dollars in government support being supplied to A.I.G., things are looking much worse for the financial world. The crisis has spread beyond the subprime market and, in many ways, beyond the mortgage market in general. As we have become more aware of the crisis through these public bank failures and the decline of the American market, it is important that we do not forget the individuals who are most directly affected, those who are facing eviction. Without certainty for the future and with the threat of losing their own "American Dream," many may find themselves taking drastic measures to keep their homes or protect their families.        / END

## Notes

[1] "Mortgage," Investorwords.com, http://www.investorwords.com/3124/mortgage.html (accessed August 15, 2008).

[2] John Kiff and Paul Mills "Money for Nothing and Checks for Free: Recent Developments in U.S. Subprime Mortgage Markets" (July 2007): 8.

[3] Ellen Schloemer et al. "Losing Ground: Foreclosures in the Subprime Market and Their Cost to Homeowners" (December 2006): 5.

[4] Schloemer, 22.

[5] Schloemer, 7.

[6] Christopher L. Foote, et al. "Subprime Facts: What (We Think) We Know about the Subprime Crisis and What We Don't" (May 2008): 32.

[7] Souphala Chomsisengphet and Anthony Pennington-Cross, "The Evolution of the Subprime Mortgage Market" Federal Reserve Bank of St. Louis Review (January/February 2006): 38.

[8] Schloemer, 7

[9] Center for Responsible Lending. "Subprime Lending: A Net Drain in Home-ownership" (March 2007): 3.

[10] Foote, 40.

[11] Schloemer, 11

[12] Community Investment Network. "Predatory Lending Overview" (April 2006): 1.

[13] Community Investment Network, 1.

[14] Schloemer, 5

[15] Elizabeth Renuart "An Overview of the Predatory Mortgage Lending Process" (2004): 470.

[16] Schloemer, 5

[17] Schloemer, 28

[18] Schloemer, 24.

[19] Foote, 13.

[20] Foote, 13.

[21] Foote, 13.

[22] Foote, 13.

[23] James H. Carr and Lopa Kolluri. "Predatory Lending: An Overview" (2001): 1-2.

[24] Carr, 2.

[25] Foote, 4.

[26] Foote, 33.

[27] Schloemer, 8.

[28] Foote, 46.

[29] Schloemer, 4.

[30] Schloemer, 7.

[31] Schloemer, 7.

[32] Schloemer, 7.

[33] Alain de Serres and Florian Pelgrin. "The Decline in Private Saving Rates in the 1990s in OECD Countries: How Much Can Be Explained by Non-Wealth Determinants?" (2003): 118.

[34] De Serres, 136.

[35] De Serres, 136.

[36] Foote, 27.

[37] Foote, 27.

[38] Foote, 19.

[39] Foote, 22.

[40] Schloemer, 13.

[41] Foote, 28.

[42] Hanratty, 12.

[43] Schloemer, 29.

[44] Cameron L. Cowan. "Hearing on Protecting Homeowners: Preventing Abusive Lending While Preserving Access to Credit". American Securitization Forum (November 5, 2003): 2.

[45] Richard Tomlinson and David Evans. "CDO Boom Masks Subprime Losses, Abetted by S&P, Moody's, Fitch" (May 2007): 5.

[46] Cowan, 2.

[47] Cowan, 6.

[48] Cowan, 7.

[49] Tomlinson: 6, 4.

[50] Schloemer, 29.

[51] Schloemer, 29.

[52] Patricia Hanratty and Joanne G. McClatchy. "The Neighborhood Stabilization Program" (March 2008): 14.

[53] Schloemer, 22.

[54] Center for Responsible Lending, 2.

[55] Center for Responsible Lending, 3.

[56] Center for Responsible Lending, 3.

[57] Dan Immergluck and Geoff Smith. "The External Costs of Foreclosure: The Impact of Single-Family Mortgage Foreclosures on Property Value" (2006): 58.

[58] Schloemer, 24.

[59] Immergluck, 57, 59.

[60] Immergluck, 59.

[61] Immergluck, 59.

[62] Immergluck, 58.

[63] Immergluck, 60.

[64] Schloemer, 23.

[65] IEHI, Inc. "The Mortgage Lender Implode-O-Meter". Available at: http://ml-implode.com/index.html#lists. (2007-2008).

[66] IEHI, Inc.

[67] Tami Luhby. "Foreclosure crisis: The $4 billion fix". CNNMoney.com. Available at: http://money.cnn.com/2008/08/07/news/economy/housing_funds/index.htm?postversion=2008080712. (August 7, 2008).

[68] Luhby.

[69] Jeff Nielsen. "First Quarter 2008 Update: Reaching New Heights". Navigant Consulting (April 2008): 1.

[70] Nielsen: 1.

[71] Schloemer, 31.

[72] Foote, 4.

[73] Alan Mallach. "Tackling the Mortgage Crisis: 10 Action Steps for State Government". Restoring Prosperity Initiative from the Metropolitan Policy Program at Brookings (May 2008): 9-10.

# RELIEF
# ON THE W

Within three months of taking office, President Barak Obama announced his three-tiered housing plan. One aspect of the plan works to assist those individuals who are currently living in homes where the value of their mortgages is greater than that of their homes. This piece will help homeowners who are currently paying high interest rates on their loans because they are unable to refinance their current mortgages. These are all home-owners who are still paying off their mortgages, but could potentially be at risk of losing their homes as housing values continue to fall.

The second aspect of his program directly assists those homeowners who are currently facing the loss of their homes. It provides incentives to the banks to decrease monthly pay-ments for borrowers to levels where they can continue to pay off their loans. The current plan lays out a scheme that would provide government assistance to the bank to decrease a borrower's monthly payments only after the bank has decreased payments to equal 38 percent of the owner's gross monthly income. Ideally, the mortgage holder would deter-mine that the costs of foreclosure are greater than the costs of rewriting the mortgage and this would assist in keeping families in their homes.

Finally, President Obama's plan includes $200 billion of funding for Fannie Mae and Freddie Mac as an attempt to help provide additional funds for loans to be originated in the months to come.

The program has some strong aspects as well as a few faults. The program is specifically written to assist those owners who live in their homes, not people who have purchased multiple properties with the hopes of reselling them for profit. These owner-occupied

# PRESIDENT OBAMA'S HOUSING PLAN

## SIDEBAR TO MORTGAGE ARTICLE

### JESSICA HERRMANN

properties are the ones that deserve assistance, since foreclosure on these homes will result in a greater number of families without residence.

In addition, the program takes into account the need to work with servicers and the fact that mortgages have been sold to the secondary market. This has been one of the largest challenges facing homeowners today, since they cannot determine the true holder of their mortgage to renegotiate the terms of the mortgage. President Obama's plan allows the servicer the right to rewrite the mortgage without the threat of being sued by their investors.

In terms of faults in this program, there are two main problems. The first is that the plan does not deal with second mortgages. Given that the majority of the properties in foreclosure had second mortgages, the exclusion of this aspect seems important to note. Even if the first mortgages are restructured to allow the borrower to continue his/her payments, it is possible that the second mortgage will have monthly payments that are still too high for the borrower.

In addition, this plan does not consider what will happen when the house values begin to rise. If a bank restructures a borrower's mortgage to keep the family in their home and in doing so is willing to decrease the principal on the loan and then the house value increases, the borrower will currently receive the added value to the home. However, if a bank has decreased the principal, it can be argued that the bank deserves some piece of the increased value of the home. This will become an issue in the coming years when property values rise and homeowners who received restructured loans as a result of this plan begin to sell their properties.

The complexities involved in the current foreclosure crisis make it nearly impossible to structure a plan that effectively addresses every aspect of the problem. The Obama Administration has provided a basic structure to begin to assist distressed homeowners. It is not perfect, but it is a strong start.

/ END

# PAKISTA

Nichole Sobecki (EPIIC'06, Exposure'05-08) covers Turkey for *GlobalPost*. A graduate of Tufts University, she took six months away from her studies to work as a correspondent for the *Daily Star*, Lebanon's English language news-paper based in Beirut. During that time she covered an uprising at Nahr al-Bared refugee camp where Islamic militants fought a violent and lengthy battle against the Lebanese Army. She also shot and edited "The Luckiest Man: Gun Violence in Urban America," a documentary, and "Shooting for Peace," which explores several grassroots initiatives to reach people affected by AIDS, unsanitary water conditions, and civil war in Uganda. In 2008, she traveled to Pakistan where she photographed the aftermath of the assassination of Benazir Bhutto and the volatile tribal region bordering Afghanistan.

# BETWEEN BHUTTO AND THE BORDER

## NICHOLE SOBECKI

"Since the birth of Pakistan, crisis has followed crisis in rapid escalation. Millions of lives were sacrificed to create this country. Pakistan is said to be the dream of Mohammad Iqbal and the creation of Muhammad Ali Jinnah, the Quaid-e-Azam. Was anything wrong with the dream or with the one who made the dream come true?"

-

*Zulfikar Ali Bhutto,*
written in a 1978 letter to his daughter

Since its initial birthing pains – gaining independence through a brutal war with India – Pakistan has faced innumerable challenges: four coups in its 60 years of independence, rampant corruption, and waves of economic and political unrest. But the last two years have been tumultuous even by Pakistan's standards.

Once described by President Eisenhower as 'the most allied of US allies,' today Pakistan is a state riven with conflict. Pakistan's wide, largely ungoverned tribal areas have become an untouchable base for Islamic militants to attack Americans and Afghans across the border. Inside the tribal areas, Taliban warlords have taken near-total control, pushing aside the Pakistani government and imposing their own brutal form of Islam. On top of that, the country has a substantial arsenal of nuclear weapons and is in a constant state of tension with India.

There have been some changes. It's fledgling civilian government, the first since 1999, is being led by Asif Ali Zardari, who was elected based on a tide of emotions that swept the country after his famously popular wife, Benazir Bhutto, was killed by a bomb at a campaign rally. And then there is the Obama Administration's new policy toward Afghanistan and Pakistan that plans to hurl a lifeline towards Zardari.

Without doubt difficult security calculations remain. But from the peddler in Karachi to Washington's elite, there remains a common interest: to avoid a failed Pakistani state.

1 . PAKISTAN, JANUARY 2008.
A billboard, featuring the former opposition leader Benazir Bhutto, leader of the Pakistan People's party, seen in the Liari district of Pakistan's largest and most populated city, Karachi.

2 . PAKISTAN, JANUARY 2008.

A boy stands in a market in the Liari district of Karachi. Pakistan, once described by President Eisenhower as 'the most allied of US allies,' is today one of the poorest nuclear-armed states and riven with conflict. Created in 1947, upon Partition of the British Raj, as a homeland for the Indian Muslims, over the years the country has become an Islamic state. A frontline ally in the US-led war on terror, Pakistan also faces Islamist terrorism on its own soil.

3 . PAKISTAN, JANUARY 2008.
The defaced image of former opposition leader Benazir Bhutto attached to the back of a rickshaw in Karachi. The Taliban follows a ferociously literal interpretation of Islam that prohibits the depiction of faces in illustration or photograph. These strictures are often carried over into the public sphere in the form of scratched out movie and political posters.

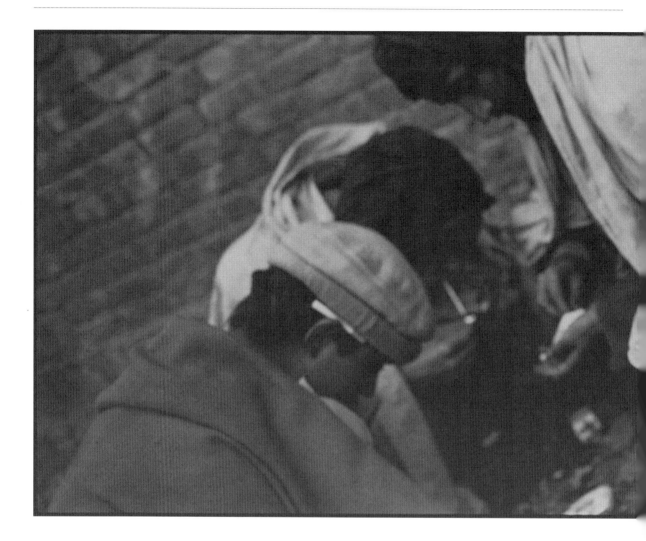

4 . PAKISTAN, JANUARY 2008.

Heroin addicts outside of Peshawar. Pakistan has some of the highest rates of addiction to heroin in the world and, in Peshawar, the smuggling of heroin and hashish is a major part of the local economy in the city. During the 1980s the torrent of heroin transformed Pakistan into a "narco-state", with heroin profits making military intelligence independent of central control. Today, with an arms pipeline going in and a drugs pipeline coming out of Afghanistan, Pakistan continues to suffer the effects of the legacy of conflict in the region.

**5 . PAKISTAN, JANUARY 2008.**

Men pray at a mosque in the center of Peshawar. With over 99 percent of the population of Peshawar Muslim, the nature of the city is overwhelmingly Islamic. Outside of the majority, who practice a peaceful adherence to an Islamic faith, there exists a darker undercurrent. Situated near the eastern end of the Khyber Pass, Peshawar is a gateway from Pakistan to Afghanistan. As the administrative center for the Federally Administered Tribal Areas (FATA), an area that has been used by the Taliban to regroup, reorganize and rearm, Peshawar heralds a contradictory role in Pakistan's turbulent political make-up.

DISCOURSE

PAKISTAN
BETWEEN BHUTTO AND THE BORDER

NICHOLE SOBECKI

103

12 OF 26

6 . PAKISTAN, JANUARY 2008.
A man stands in an alley where trash is being burned in the Liari district of Karachi, Pakistan, where supporters of Benazir Bhutto, the opposition leader, had taken to the street after her assassination.

7 . PAKISTAN, JANUARY 2008.
A group of women walk through an alley where trash was being burned in the Liari district of Karachi, Pakistan.

8 . PAKISTAN, JANUARY 2008.
A man files the barrel of a gun at a gun market in the Federally Administered Tribal Areas
(FATA). A print of Saddam Hussein in uniform hangs on the wall behind him.

DISCOURSE

PAKISTAN
BETWEEN BHUTTO AND THE BORDER

NICHOLE SOBECKI

109

18 OF 26

9 . PAKISTAN, JANUARY 2008.
A man sits in a gun market in the Federally Administered Tribal Areas (FATA). A guard stands outside the market stall holding a rifle.

DISCOURSE

PAKISTAN
BETWEEN BHUTTO AND THE BORDER

NICHOLE SOBECKI

111

20 OF 26

DISCOURSE

PAKISTAN
BETWEEN BHUTTO AND THE BORDER

NICHOLE SOBECKI

113

22 OF 26

10 . PAKISTAN, JANUARY 2008.
A gun merchant tests a weapon at a gun market in the Federally Administered Tribal Areas (FATA), whose lawlessness is affecting nearby Peshawar.

11 . PAKISTAN, JANUARY 2008.
An Afghan mother and child on the road outside of Peshawar. After the Soviet invasion of Afghanistan in 1979 Peshawar served as a political centre for anti-Soviet Mujahideen, and was surrounded by huge camps of Afghan refugees. Peshawar managed to assimilate many of the Pashtun Afghan refugees, while many other Afghan refugees remained in camps awaiting a possible return to Afghanistan.

12 . PAKISTAN, JANUARY 2008.
A boy runs through a cemetery on the outskirts of Peshawar holding a kite. In Persian "Pesh-awar" means high fortress and, as the Islamic insurgency pours out of the adjacent tribal regions into the city, Peshawar is becoming increasingly important not only to the future of Pakistan but equally to the success of the US-bolstered Karzai regime in Afghanistan.

DISCOURSE

PAKISTAN
BETWEEN BHUTTO AND THE BORDER

NICHOLE SOBECKI

117

26 OF 26

# THE EVE
# OF OUR L
# ELEGY FO
# AKONYI

SAMUEL JAMES

DISCOURSE

**THE EVENING OF OUR LIVES**
ELEGY FOR AKONYI BEDO

SAMUEL JAMES

119

2 OF 8

NING
IVES
R
EDO

Samuel James is a senior at Tufts University in the combined degree program with the School of Museum of Fine Arts Boston. He is a member of the inaugural class of Synaptic Scholars of the Institute for Global Leadership, Tufts University, as well as a member of the Institute's photojournalism and human rights group EXPOSURE.

Samuel spent the 2007-2008 academic year in Lagos, Nigeria researching the megacity as his Synaptic project and participated in the 2008 EXPOSURE-Aftermath photojournalism workshop in Northern Uganda.

-

Throughout the course of 22 years of conflict in Northern Uganda, Lazarus Nyero never left home. His village hut was not burned, unlike nearly every other hut in the area. He was never harmed, unlike the tens of thousands killed and maimed. The conflict uprooted nearly 1.9 million people, who fled their villages to sprawling camps for Internally Displaced Persons (IDPs). For more than 15 years, Lazarus lived in isolation.

Like his father, and many generations before him, Lazarus was born in Akonyi Bedo, a small Acholi village located 15 kilometers outside of Gulu town. Like his father, he was a farmer. His plot produced beans, maize, sugar cane and groundnuts. Next to his hut was a mango tree, which produced fruit for his family and shade for his visitors. He built the home with his hands. He has lived there for 73 years.

In the late 1980s, the Lord's Resistance Army (LRA) began attacking civilians and abducting children. By the mid-1990s, Akonyi Bedo was abandoned, with most residents relocating to the nearby Unyama IDP camp. The LRA rebels came to Lazarus' home often, demanding to know where the government soldiers were located. He did not know. They left him.

He had a family. His wife passed away at a young age. Of his four children, some were abducted, some returned.

In 2004, the Ugandan Army forced Lazarus to move closer to the village's main road, where his safety could be better monitored by government troops who were assigned to protect the area. During this time, his original home was demolished, not by LRA attacks, but by termites.

He has never seen money, but maintains himself with quiet dignity. He keeps his one pair of nice shoes on a shelf in his hut. They are creased and weathered, but shined. On his straw mat, he keeps a neatly folded, thread bare blanket. He uses a rope to hold up his oversized trousers. His bones are fragile and his skin loose. His face is carved with deep crevices and his eyes burn like black embers.

"I am the winner," he says. He knows survival.

When he can, he sips the local 'dry water,' a potent local gin made with fermented cassava. Adong, his 70-year old neighbor, serves him a glass. Adong only recently returned to the village after many years in the Unyama camp. Back in the village she spends her days brewing gin and tending to small children. She laughs as the baby in her lap tries to suck her breast. "I am dry," she chuckles. Her dress stays loose, occasionally revealing ancient traces of motherhood. She pours herself a hot glass as well.

These are the elderly. Since the conflict ceasefire, they are the first to return home to the land that nurtured them.

They enjoy simple pleasures. They are forever patient. But life is ephemeral. When a neighbor dies, they come together to fulfill their obligations.

In Acholiland, safe passage for the deceased is not ensured until three nights after the body is placed in the earth. Three nights after the death of a neighbor, Lazarus, Adong and the other village elders trek through the bush to join the family in mourning. They arrive as the sun sets. Adong sits on the floor with the other women. Lazurus takes a chair. With one cup and a large plastic jug, they share dry water until their minds are thoroughly engulfed by memories. Elderly men take turns beating cowhide drums with heavy wooden sticks. Elderly women scrape gourds across a log. They all sing.

With slow, wobbly steps and shuffles, they gather around the drummer. Lazarus gradually rises from his chair and joins the rickety group of dancing elders. Though his fragile frame can no longer keep up with the frenetic Acholi stomp, his movements are graceful and composed. Without losing a step, he grabs his staff and triumphantly raises it to the heavens.

So much depends on the rhythm. Singing turns to shrieking, which in turn leads to more stomping. Periodically while dancing, old women tilt their heads back and wail into the sky. The tears flow deep into the night, but the bodies do not stop swaying to the drum. Joy and sorrow blend in the stomp. This is the release. With sweat and tears, the Acholi confront death and celebrate life. The stomping continues until old bones can no longer stand straight.

For 22 years, the Acholi were unable to perform their cultural obligations to the dead. During the conflict, a body could sometimes be transported to the village during the day and quickly buried without ceremony. More commonly, the elders would be forced to conduct haphazard ceremonies within cramped and foreign IDP camps.

But now, they can resume their duties. Sipping dry water in the twilight, exhausted elders huddle around a small bonfire, discussing the legacy of their culture. For the first time in nearly two decades they can feel free to pass the night in the village and properly celebrate their deceased brothers and sisters. But what is missing is that which has always been missing since the conflict. The youth have not returned.

Abducted, displaced and uprooted, the youth remain scattered. Many have spent their entire lives in IDP camps. They have no connection to the land that nurtured the generations before them. This distresses the elders, whose duty it is to preserve and pass on the culture. But the youth are not around.

An ancient face around the fire proclaims, "This is the evening of our lives. The hours are weak. Let us not allow our culture to fade away into the night." They discuss until the new day arrives.

For Lazarus, it is the same as any day. Using his walking staff, he slowly eases himself from the wooden chair where he passed the night. One by one with trembling fingers, he fastens the buttons of the coarse canvas jacket covering his bare chest. The youth have not returned. Like so many days before, he quietly resumes the solitary march to his field.

/ END

**PHOTO CAPTIONS : LEFT TO RIGHT, TOP TO BOTTIOM.**
LAZARUS NYERO. AGE 73. OF THE VILLAGE OF AKONYI BEDO IN NORTHERN UGANDA.
AFTER THE DEATH OF AN ELDER IN AKONYI BEDO. THE BODY IS TRANSPORTED TO THE BURIAL SITE.
THE VILLAGE PREPARES FOR THE BURIAL CEREMONY.
/
THE CASKET IS PREPARED FOR BURIAL.
THE DECEASED IS BURIED WITH HIS ANCESTORS IN THE FAMILY COMPOUND.
IN ANTICIPATION FOR THE BURIAL CEREMONY. GLASSES OF LOCAL BREW ARE SHARED AMONG THE VILLAGE ELDERS.

DISCOURSE

THE EVENING OF OUR LIVES
ELEGY FOR AKONYI BEDO

SAMUEL JAMES

123

6 OF 8

PHOTO CAPTIONS : LEFT TO RIGHT, TOP TO BOTTIOM.
A WOMAN MOURNS THE DEATH OF HER HUSBAND.
VILLAGE ELDERS DANCE AROUND A CEREMONIAL FIRE. CELEBRATING THEIR DECEASED BROTHER'S SUCCESSFUL TRANSITION BACK INTO THE EARTH.
WOMEN PREPARE MILLET THE MORNING AFTER THE BURIAL CEREMONY.
/
THE MORNING AFTER THE BURIAL CEREMONY. LAZARUS RETURNS TO HIS FIELD.
LAZARUS' SHADOW.
EVENING FALLS ON THE VILLAGE OF AKONYI BEDO.

DISCOURSE

THE EVENING OF OUR LIVES
ELEGY FOR AKONYI BEDO

SAMUEL JAMES

125

8 OF 8

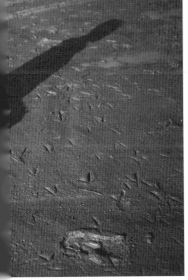

# MATO OPUT

RETHINKING
TRANSITIONAL JUSTICE
IN NORTHERN UGANDA

JESSICA ANDERSON

Jessica Anderson (EPIIC'06) is the co-founder and director of Collaborative Transitions Africa, an organization dedicated to collaborating with traditional leaders, academic institutions and grassroots organizations to facilitate support for local initiatives. She has primarily focused on restorative justice mechanisms in Northern Uganda for the past several years. A 2008 graduate of Tufts University, she conducted field research pertaining to issues of conflict, GBV and transitional justice in Ghana, South Africa, and Uganda. She is currently a research associate with Pragmora: Building the Peace and a private contractor with the Pearson Peacekeeping Centre. Next year she will be a Rotary Scholar at the University of Witswatersrand in South Africa for a masters program in security sector reform.

Preface

I am in Uganda, a country on the cusp of resolving a brutal and unrelenting civil war, and for the past month I have been interviewing politicians, academics, NGO's, and war-affected men and women. My goal is to understand how they envision post-conflict justice, with a focus on Northern civilians who have been displaced by the conflict.

My translator guides me into a camp on the outskirts of Gulu Town on the back of his boda-boda, bringing me to an internally displaced persons (IDP) settlement in Northern Uganda. On this rain-soaked summer morning, I find a dozen men and women spread out on mats and rickety eucalyptus stools looking at me expectantly. In spite of the butterflies in my stomach, my first interview begins. It is with Melie, a young mother of seven who has lived in Palenga camp since 1996, after being forcibly displaced by the Ugandan People's Defence Force (UPDF), the Ugandan army. Melie is soft-spoken and shy, cradling a sleeping girl in her arms while another baby is strapped to her back and wailing unapologetically. As she bounces her newborn son into a soft whimper, I ask Melie what a normal day is like for her in the camp. She replies :

-

In the evenings, when I go to bathe, I start to worry. They can burn you while you're sleeping. 'When are we going to get out?' you ask. 'Will it ever change? Am I going to be here forever?' These are the questions that haunt you and don't let you sleep. When it reaches morning, you need to ask for the nearest land to cultivate. There isn't enough to eat and the food rations aren't enough. We need to cultivate. After the field, we get water, firewood, cook the meals, and look after the children. Once the evening comes, I just start to worry again.[1]

-

Melie has not been abducted or mutilated. She hasn't lost any close family members, and she does not fall into any of the "extremely vulnerable" categories that have become so fashionable among humanitarian organizations today. Melie is one Acholi woman, among the 1.7 million displaced in Northern Uganda, and she lives in a state of perpetual fear and deprivation in Palenga. With the simple description of her day, I learned that suffering is pervasive here, even in the absence of physical wounds.

Through Melie I discovered the importance of thinking about more subtle violence lying below the conflict radar. These structural forms of violence and insecurity are not being addressed in the conflict zone, despite the fact that nearly everyone in Northern Uganda is affected. Since the level of impact is broad, silent, and pervasive, it is more difficult to tackle and is often ignored. It does not seem as if these difficulties should necessarily pave the way to paralysis; instead, more attention should be paid to the intricacies of violence. For a woman like Melie, deprivation and the chronic threat of physical violence create a steady state of insecurity. Daily life is focused on surviving instead of thriving, and so Melie focuses her attention on the incremental – on waking up in the morning and staying alive – instead of planning for her future. She is forced to compartmentalize her life, and focus on making it day by day in the terrible conditions of IDP camps.

The questions that constantly turned over and over again in my mind while in the camps were: What exactly could justice be in this context? How can one begin to compensate for the insecurity and want experienced by the Melies of Northern Uganda? As I discovered the many ways that violence impacts the lives of Acholis in Northern Uganda, I began to explore the other subtle, structural factors that influenced the way people lived, and how they discussed concepts of justice. Every interaction with men and women like Melie revealed that local voices are often omitted from the discourse; as a result, their desires for justice remain unnoticed as well. Any effort to restore a sense of normalcy to IDPs requires a close look at how local actors imagine justice, and how this conflicts with national and international conceptions of transitional justice.

Historical Background

Under British rule, Southern Uganda was considered an economic powerhouse while Northerners were pigeonholed as either warriors or farmers. The Southern perception of a militarized North eventually became reality. By the outbreak of World War II, more Acholi men were serving in the army than any other ethnic group in Uganda. Colonial rule ended and Northerner Milton Obote assumed power in 1960, relying heavily on the Northerner-dominant army to maintain his rule of Uganda. Southerner Idi Amin launched a military coup against Obote in 1971, and his rule was marked by gross human rights abuses, especially against supporters of Obote. Amin was then overthrown in 1979.[2] Milton Obote returned to power in 1979. In 1985, Yoweri Museveni began a guerrilla war and his National Resistance Army assumed power and he assumed the presidency of Uganda in January 1986.

Upon Museveni's accession, Alice Lakwena launched the Holy Spirit Movement (HSM) as a religious response to the political tensions and widespread discontent with Museveni between the Acholi and other Northern ethnic groups. Lakwena's alleged cousin, Joseph Kony, assumed control of the military movement in 1988. Kony currently leads what is now known as The Lord's Resistance Army (LRA), a rebel guerrilla army operating mainly in

DISCOURSE

MATO OPUT
RETHINKING TRANSITIONAL JUSTICE
IN NORTHERN UGANDA

JESSICA ANDERSON

129

4 OF 12

Northern Uganda, the Democratic Republic of the Congo, and Southern Sudan.[3] Support for the LRA from Lakwena's supporters dwindled as violence increased, and the LRA began resorting to the abduction of men and women from their homes in order to fill the rebel ranks. The government continued with its military response to the civil war, and in 1996 it began creating 'protected villages' into which some Northern Ugandans fled voluntarily, and others were forcibly displaced by the UPDF. This forcible displacement further deepened the antagonistic attitude that many Acholi have toward the government, especially as the population faced continued attacks by the LRA, despite living in "protected" camps. In March 2002, the UPDF launched Operation Iron Fist against the LRA, which led to more destruction and devastation than ever was seen before in the conflict. As a result, President Museveni referred the LRA to the International Criminal Court (ICC) as a terrorist group guilty of international war crimes in December 2003.

## The Rule of Law Within The Current Crisis

The Government of Uganda (GoU) has maintained a military strategy for tackling the Lord's Resistance Army, creating a scenario in which civilians face threats from both LRA and UPDF forces. The intent of the IDP camps was to shield Northern Ugandans from LRA attacks, but massive levels of displacement have created new and potentially more serious protection problems for IDPs – with the perpetrators often being the very UPDF forces sent to protect the displaced from the LRA insurgency. In a recent study, IDPs reported that UPDF mobile units are the most notorious for committing violent abuses against civilians. These abuses include, but are not limited to: "attacking civilians pursuing livelihood activities in the cleared zones, raping civilian women pursuing livelihood activities, assaulting and raping civilians found in breach of curfews, killing civilians in camps arising from disputes, and torture during detention."[4] As militarization continues, the rule of law is conspicuously absent from the North, and the disconnect between the government and the North is even wider in light of the UPDF's behavior. Even though the aim of transitional justice is to seek accountability for conflict atrocities, the GoU refuses to admit its role in the civil war.

In lieu of a legitimate rule of law process, the UPDF has responded by creating local militias and local defense units (LDU) to fill the vacuum of order and control in the IDP camps. This civilian protection strategy has flooded the region with small arms, creating local armies with no formal accountability in which, "They themselves prey on the vulnerable and are exploited by the powerful."[5] Salary payments often never arrive, and the militias exert their power by stealing food and goods from the community, especially from more vulnerable groups such as child-headed households and war orphans. Meanwhile, camps containing tens of thousands of people do not have a single police officer to monitor, investigate, or prosecute crimes. According to estimates, the total population deprived of police easily exceeds one million.[6] The "protection strategy," an irresponsible substitute for proper policing forces, instead puts the burden of security on civilians who are potentially raising arms against their own children, brothers, sisters, and friends in the LRA ranks. The current militias were also hurriedly recruited, poorly screened, and incompletely trained. Many young men feel frustrated with the idleness and deprivation they face in the camps and join the militia as a response. The North is confronted with a situation in which everyone faces a steady state of insecurity and fear as thousands of weapons are distributed to groups of displaced, uneducated, unemployed men who have little to lose.

The justice system in Northern Uganda is similarly dysfunctional. According to a Ugandan researcher in Gulu :

-

The criminal justice system right now is terrible. There aren't enough judges, there isn't enough infrastructure. If you want to create security post-conflict, you need these elements! Right now there are 4,000 cases of sexual violence in Gulu waiting to go forward, and I just don't think they ever will.

-

As he describes, there is no relief from the insecurity in Northern Uganda. Internally displaced persons are confronted with the security threat of the militias, the UPDF soldiers, and the LRA rebels, and live with a virtually collapsed court structure. "In Northern Uganda, where the protective system provided by the state has failed, it is the civilians themselves who are forced to find ways of 'coping' with their situation."[7] The state continues to deny or underplay the negative impact of its own forces, undermining the pain caused by UPDF soldiers and further blocking trust in the state.

One of the most embedded and lingering effects of the humanitarian crisis that will inevitably carry over into the peace process is the Acholis' extreme mistrust of their government. A professor of Peace and Conflict at Makerere University described his conception of transitional justice: "The long-term goals are good governance, respect of human rights, respect of the constitution. But right now there's a lack of respect for the state. We need participatory democracy and national unity."[8] For Professor Nkabahona, transitional justice is the rule of law, and yet the North-South disconnect is such that by having a perceived 'other' for the Acholis to resent, their own identity and sense of alienation has become more clearly defined over the course of the conflict. For many Acholis, the real aims of the GoU's inaction are perceived to be revenge against Northerners for past crimes and ensuring that the North does not pose any political challenge to the current national power structure."[9] Acholi indignity at such an agenda creates a social situation in which the government is seen as an obstacle to peace and far removed from the protective role it should play for its citizens.

As for national trials as a rule-of-law-promoting transitional justice measure, a common opinion echoed in Gulu and Kampala was: "It will look like the Government of Uganda is essentially trying the Acholi people – tribalizing the conflict. As if all that we have are Acholis killing Acholis."[10] Acholis are thus often unwilling to trust the government to hold national trials, which is a common reaction when, "citizens view legal institutions skeptically because of corruption, systematic bias, association with abusive past regimes."[11] As a Kampala-based NGO director candidly informed me, "Kampala is three hours away from Gulu. Here we spend our nights in discos. But supposedly there is an official structure called Uganda."[12] Such a disconnect, riddled with biases and abuse, demonstrates the importance of nationally reforming police, court, and justice structures through a protracted and politically-willed process, which can also constitute a form of transitional justice. However, this does not tackle the rule of law in the short-term, in a context where accountability structures are virtually nonexistent. In light of a history of exclusion, minimal trust in state institutions, and diverse every day realities, short term rule of law measures such as trials will be difficult to implement successfully.

## The International Criminal Court

As mentioned above, President Museveni asked the International Criminal Court to release indictments against the Lord's Resistance Army in 2003, following the UPDF's failure to stop the rebellion through military means. In light of national-level failure, the ICC presents an opportunity for the international community to hold the LRA responsible for mass violations of human rights and crimes against humanity. However, the methods of the ICC alienate many Northern Ugandans, who are put off by its "straightjacket notion of justice, one sided and alien to Africa as it is."[13]

### UPDF Impunity

Despite the ICC's status as an accountability mechanism, it does not necessarily resonate in a meaningful way with Acholis on the ground in Northern Uganda. "Real equality before the law requires courts that are strong and independent enough to enforce it."[14] However, by focusing indictments exclusively on the LRA, the ICC is seen as biased and cannot enforce the law for crimes and atrocities committed by the Ugandan state. According to James Otto, director of Human Rights Focus based in Gulu, "The ICC has dented its own image in not investigating the Ugandan government which has also committed atrocities."[15] Beyond the ICC's image, denial of the crimes of the UPDF is often con-

# HOWEVER, BY FOCUSING INDICTMENTS EXCLUSIVELY ON THE LRA, THE ICC IS SEEN AS BIASED AND CANNOT ENFORCE THE LAW FOR CRIMES AND ATROCITIES COMMITTED BY THE UGANDAN STATE.

strued as an attack against the Acholi people in the North. The ICC is thus considered illegitimate by many Acholis because it does not address the reality of their experience and many perceive it as a roadblock to the peace process. By failing to address the role of the UPDF, the ICC allows for no real equality before the law, and the success of the ICC in promoting the rule of law is thereby undermined in the region.

### Root Causes and the Retributive
In addition to denying the UPDF's role in the conflict, the ICC practices retributive justice, or "Western justice." In the North, the ICC's narrow mandate of holding only a few leaders accountable is often considered irrelevant in addressing the root causes of the civil war. According to a Kampala-based NGO director, "The ICC is a seed for more conflict. At what point are we going to address the historical contexts of these leaders? The ICC is a quick fix to a very complicated problem."[16] Just as Uganda is limited by a complex social, political and economic web, so are the decisions of its leaders. Most IDPs are more interested in addressing the deeper, underlying causes of the conflict than simply bringing top LRA leaders to trial. International justice "displaces alternative visions of social justice that are less individualistic and more focused on communities and responsibilities."[17] The ICC fails to look holistically at the economic marginalization, ethnic prejudices, and political violence that have pervaded Northern Uganda's history. A legal specialist in Gulu lamented the "magic

bullet" approach of the ICC, and its potential to falsely convince people that an answer has been found. "Uganda as a concept has always interfered with people's lives. Wars after wars after wars. If we think that a couple rebels on trial will heal this problem we are deceiving ourselves."[18]

Peace as Justice

It is apparent that a deeper look at the conflict – and more than "a couple rebels on trial"– is needed to pursue transitional justice and reestablish the rule of law in Northern Uganda. In particular, emphasizing physical violence is problematic when 1.7 million people have been displaced from their homes and forced to live in devastating conditions of material deprivation without health care or sanitation. According to a researcher based in Kampala, "To the extent that people think it's Kony and Museveni fighting this war, they're mistaken. It's millions of IDPs, abductees, and local militias."[19] A system of justice that focuses on individual accountability not only misses the root causes of the conflict, but also fails to account for the importance locals place on ending to the conflict at any cost, "The desire for long-term stability outweighs the demands of modern justice as articulated in international law."[20] The Kampala-based women's organization NAWOU commented on the need for security, "Schools, hospitals, better water, that's what the other districts were asking for. In the North, they said they wanted peace. At first we thought that they didn't want to cooperate, or didn't understand. But they said to us, 'How can you ask us what we need when we can't move twenty meters?'" Stakeholders in the quest for accountability at the international level have underestimated the entire notion of peace as justice and the importance that IDPs place on a lasting end to the conflict.

By assuming that the rule of law can be established through such a narrow interpretation of accountability, the ICC ignores the complexity of the conflict. The ICC is considered problematic for both pragmatic and historical reasons. As a displaced woman in Koro camp, Gulu said, "I don't see how the ICC is going to benefit me. Is it going to build my house? Or give me seeds?"[21] Clearly, there are many issues in Uganda that run deeper than anything the ICC proposes to solve. In light of these shortcomings, the role of the ICC should be framed specifically and humbly as upholding international justice and accountability, but not necessarily as promoting justice or the rule of law on the ground in Northern Uganda. Furthermore, the ICC should be more conscious of local conceptions of justice and the real purpose of the institution's work. After all, "are these international judgments really for the survivors of war and genocide, or are they for some more lofty, albeit important cause of 'international justice'?"[22] The realities on the ground seem to indicate the latter – this is not necessarily wrong, but it must be widely understood in the region, and international justice must not be billed as something that it is not. Now, the task is to think about how justice and the rule of law should look in the short term, if national and international measures have been found inadequate.

# "Are these international judgments really for the survivors of war and genocide, or are they for some more lofty, albeit important cause of 'international justice'?"

## Mato Oput

Jeroen de Zeeuw highlights the key pitfalls of both the ICC and GoU in approaching the rule of law and justice, "Post-war communities need to define and take ownership of the process of justice... Individuals and groups crave respect, acknowledgement, and affirmation. They want to be involved in decisions that affect their lives, and they resent being treated as the object of some other body's plans."[23] In resistance to being treated as "the object of some other body's plans," support for the widespread use of the Acholi justice mechanism of Mato Oput has increased steadily in the region. The main objective of the Mato Oput ritual is to reintegrate a perpetrator (historically, someone who murdered a person from another clan) into the community with their victim, through a process of "establishing truth, confession, reparation, repentance, and forgiveness."[24] It is a way for locals to exercise their agency and control over the process, which is critical for the legitimacy of any justice practice. "Although law and order might appear to be a universal good, it also depends heavily on citizens' acceptance of laws and on the government's legitimacy to make laws that bind them."[25] This disconnect between law and local legitimacy was evident in my interview with a *New Vision* journalist :

-

Does the ICC really bring peace? My nose has been cut off but I'm the one calling for Mato Oput. It is me who has been tortured. But we just want these children to grow well. We

know culturally what to do with these people when they're brought back home. Let them all come back and we will handle them.[26]
-

Kleinfeld supports this sort of flexibility and claims that whether the restraining powers are legal, moral or constitutional, is unimportant. Rather, the effectiveness of the process is what matters. If Mato Oput is effective in achieving a sense of justice, and resonates with war-affected people on the ground, then it should be supported as such.

There is a willingness in the region for the process of Mato Oput to adapt to the specific context of the war. "Dialoguing is the key to the restoration of broken communities. Yes, Mato Oput. But it often doesn't matter what you do. Dialoguing is key, though. Northern ethnicities are communal in nature. We need to interact, to talk with each other."[27] Sally Engle Merry makes a parallel observation, writing that "local cultural practices are far more fluid and open to change than the essentialized model suggests."[28] Religious and cultural leaders have discussed this fluidity, and many support Mato Oput's restorative conceptions of justice in a broader sense, where "restoring perpetrators back into harmony with the values of the community is one component of justice."[29] From these observations it is apparent that moral values and the quest for justice is still the primary aim, but that the process can take many, varied forms.

It appears that the underlying values of Mato Oput – not every detail of the historical ritual – are most valuable in Northern Uganda. As Archbishop Odama claims, "It's restorative healing for both sides, and saving. We feel it's better than just going into court. The purpose of Mato Oput is conciliatory. It will stop the crime from being repeated and this will never happen again."[30] The rule of law is thus promoted in keeping with a history of the practice, while restoring the community's relationships in a way that may be more valuable in the aftermath of violent conflict. Furthermore, the communal nature of the practice is seen as a form of accountability in itself, since there is consensus in decision-making and outcomes that are distinct from the seemingly arbitrary nature of trials. "Unlike the current legal system, the perpetrator is charged for what he has done and confesses. If you refuse that you have done anything, you would lose your place in society. It's not just lawyers playing their cards."[31] Mato Oput is positioned to be an inclusive justice process that provides local-level accountability and avoids the skepticism that Northerners have towards lawyers and the national court structures.

While current international and national mechanisms are lacking on the ground, there is evidence that locals in Northern Uganda are enthusiastic about supporting Mato Oput as a justice mechanism. Mato Oput addresses issues of restoration and unification of the community and is rooted in a historical process that resonates in a more meaningful way with locals than national court processes or the ICC. It also allows for flexibility in the justice process that is absent from these two mechanisms. Furthermore, as a locally owned process, Mato Oput is less likely to fall prey to the feelings of alienation and distrust that are currently ubiquitous in Northern Uganda. By promoting local agency, local desires

DISCOURSE

MATO OPUT
RETHINKING TRANSITIONAL JUSTICE
IN NORTHERN UGANDA

JESSICA ANDERSON

135

10 OF 12

and values become central to short-term post-conflict stabilization. With Mato Oput, those who have lived and endured through Uganda's civil war have the opportunity to provide a more nuanced and honest look at the conflict, as well as post-conflict justice.

Mato Oput is not a magic bullet for reestablishing the rule of law in Northern Uganda. Rather, it is the sole justice and accountability measure that is widely understood at the local level, and of which there is no legacy of mistrust or abuse. There is still a need for international accountability, as well as a stable system of policing, courts, and justice structures at the national level. However, these structures may need to be built gradually. Moreover, the parameters of each mechanism should be properly understood and not expected to do more work than they are capable of delivering. Mato Oput has the potential to provide accountability and security in a setting where this has been lacking for a long time. By emphasizing local agency, those disenfranchised from the war can begin to recover from the conflict on their own terms, while other aspects of justice are addressed over time. In order to promote justice and stability – the aims of the rule of law – we need to consider both how to address past actions as well as how to move forward. Mato Oput fills a crucial role within this progression, but it will be meaningless if not surrounded by parallel measures of transitional justice and accountability for both past crimes and future offenses in Uganda.

## Conclusions

The limitations of formal justice are most vivid when there are many 'dirty hands,' as there are in civil conflicts like Northern Uganda. Justice, like beauty, is in the eye of the beholder and can be interpreted in a variety of ways. It can legitimately take many forms.

Justice, in terms of both past acts and future stability, has multiple roles, meanings, and functions in society. It is a diverse term: for many IDPs in Northern Uganda, post-conflict justice is the ability to live free of extreme material deprivation and outside a state of perpetual fear. Justice can also mean the knowledge that the conflict will end, giving hope for a better future. While the ICC has a role to play, it should be understood narrowly as a means of accountability for the perpetrators of crimes against humanity. The burden of creating institutions and mechanisms for justice lies with the Ugandan state, but when the state is incapable of establishing the rule of law – as is the case currently in Northern Uganda – local mechanisms can provide some form of accountability and justice in the region. With a forward-looking approach, rule of law and transitional justice can complement each other by reflecting on the past and promoting security in the future. In tandem with a realistic acceptance of the ICC's role, the national police forces and court system should be bolstered and improved as a form of long-term transitional justice. But in the shorter term, local practices can provide a response that both holds meaning and fulfills the aims of rule of law and transitional justice. With this conclusion, I suggest that local practices should be adopted slowly, critically, with reservation, and with the engagement of grassroots organizations and formerly displaced persons.

Northern Ugandans have a strong sense of what justice looks like. For many, it includes trials, but it can also mean peace, freedom from the terror of the IDP camps, and an end to the humiliation of eating World Food Programme handouts for over a decade. Their goal is to regain some sense of normalcy in their daily lives and to have faith in the system from which they seek justice.

Finally, in order to successfully transition from violent conflict, it is crucial to give war survivors a stake in defining justice and owning the justice process. Northern Ugandans have a strong sense of what justice looks like. For many, it includes trials, but it can also mean peace, freedom from the terror of the IDP camps, and an end to the humiliation of eating World Food Programme handouts for over a decade. Their goal is to regain some sense of normalcy in their daily lives and to have faith in the system from which they seek justice. While international and national actors have failed in this regard, local justice practices resonate with many people. If justice is not owned by the people who suffered injustice, who is it for and what is its purpose? As the resolution of Uganda's civil war remains in limbo, it is essential to solicit the post-conflict aspirations and imaginations of the war-affected. What do they dream of? What is their conception of justice, and how does this fit into national and international frameworks? Instead of discounting local ideas, which are focused on peace, security, and ending deprivation, these ideas should be embraced. Justice is in the eye of the beholder, but more attention must be paid to whose justice is taking priority in Uganda. Local voices can ultimately contribute to a more nuanced idea of justice, as well as to a more inclusive and holistic post-conflict transition. Promoting local agency paves the way for an enduring end to conflict by addressing root causes and local needs, immediate concerns and the long-term future of the Ugandan state.                                                    / END

Notes

1 Melie, personal interview. 2007.

2 Allen, Tim. War and Justice in Northern Uganda: An Assesment of the ICC's Intervention. London: London School of Economics, 2005. 28.

3 It is important to understand the international dimension of this conflict. The Ugandan government has been fighting a proxy war with Sudan by supplying the SPLA with arms. Meanwhile, the Government of Southern Sudan has been supporting the LRA in Uganda as well, with both refuge and economic support.

4 "Nowhere to Hide: Humanitarian Protection Threats in Northern Uganda." edited by Oxfam UK. Kampala: Civil Society Organizations for Peace in Northern Uganda, 2004. 89.

5 Nowhere to Hide 2003: 23.

6 Uprooted and Forgotten 2004: 44

7 Sooma 2006: 115

8 Nkabahona, Alexander. Personal interview. Kampala, Uganda. 23 July 2007.

9 In Search of Security: A Regional Analysis of Armed Conflict in Northern Uganda and Eastern Uganda and Southern Sudan." Boston: Feinstein International Center, 2005. 4.

10 Mugishe, Richard. Personal Interview. Kampala, Uganda. 23 June 2007.

11 Stromseth, Jane, David Wippman, and Rosa Brooks. Can Might Make Rights? Building the Rule of Law After Military Interventions. New York: Cambridge UP, 2006. 249.

12 Mugishe.

13 Akec, John. Ugandan Double Stand and ICC Threaten Juba Talks. Sudan Tribune. 1 October 2006. 2.

14 Kleinfeld, Rachel. Competing Definitions of the Rule of Law . Carnegie Endowment for International Peace. Carnegie Endowment, 2005. 31-62. 3 Dec. 2007. 37.

15 Otto.

16 Mugishe.

17 Merry, Sally Engle. Human Rights and Gender Violence: Translating International law into Local Justice Chicago: The University of Chicago Press, 2005. 4.

18 Tindifa, Andrew. Personal Interview. Kampala, Uganda. 12 June 2007.

19 Okello, Moses Personal Interview. Kampala, Uganda. 23 June 2007.

20 Refugee Law Project 2004: 23.

21 Harriet. Personal Interview. Gulu, Uganda. 21 July 2007.

22 Bonaifer 2005: 4.

23 Zeeuw, Jeroen de. "Building Peace in War-Torn Societies: From Concept to Strategy." Research Project on Rehabilitation and Sustainable Peace, Netherlands Institute of International Relations, 2001.12.

24 Refugee Law Project 2006: 37.

25 Kleinfeld 2006: 41.

26 Ouiwee.

27 Okello.

28 Merry 2005: 10

29 Baines, Erin. "Roco Wat I Acoli: Restoring Relationships in Acholiland: Traditional Approaches to Justice and Reintegration ": Liu Institute for Global Issues and the Gulu District NGO Forum, 2004. 23.

30 Odama, Archbishop John Baptist. Personal Interview. 10 July 2007. Gulu Archdiocese, Gulu, Uganda.

31 Ojok

# DO YOU BELIEVE SECOND CHANCES

A ROUNDTABLE DISCUSSION
INTERVIEW CONDUCTED
BY NATHANIEL TEICHMAN

# IN

Nathaniel Teichman is a senior at Tufts University majoring in International Relations. He worked as a law clerk in the Lowell Juvenile Court where he researched the School-to-Prison Pipeline along with school push out and disproportionate minority contact. He will be working with Physicians for Human Rights.

# – "Every day I've got a funeral or a wake to attend."

Teny Gross is not describing the mounting death toll in Iraq or the constant threats facing American troops in Afghanistan. Instead, Gross, a former Israeli soldier and graduate of Tufts University and Harvard Divinity School, is talking about the stark reality of a war much closer to home – the war on the inner city streets of our cities. Renowned as one of the architects of the "Boston Miracle" that radically lowered the number of homicides and violent crime in Boston, Gross has continued his work with at-risk youth in Providence, Rhode Island. Now the director of the Institute for the Study and Practice of Non-Violence, Gross leads a team of street workers, tirelessly fighting to prevent the juvenile violence that is tormenting the city of Providence. With an estimated 1,400 active gang members, Gross and his team are struggling to give kids an opportunity to rise above the violent life that surrounds them.

David Cartagena's life is a story of hope. A powerfully built man with a gentle demeanor, Cartagena knows all too well the hurdles that lay in wait for a child in Providence. Raised in a broken home, he sought the family he never had in the embrace of the Latin Kings Gang. Entrenched in gang life at an early age, he ended up on the wrong side of the law and found himself in juvenile lockup. Sitting in his cell, he needed only to look out his window to see his future. Prison guards constantly reminded him and his fellow inmates that they would end up at the adult correctional facility that stood there. According to the Rhode Island Department of Corrections, there is an approximately 46 percent recidivism rate in the state (2004 Recidivism Study: Two-Year Follow-Up by Bree E Derrick and Greg McCarthy, August 2007), of which Cartagena was all too aware. The trend of recidivism is a disturbing one that is not only disrupting life in Providence, but also affecting the nation as a whole. After several arrests and lockups, Cartagena fought through his dire circumstances and dedicated his life to helping others

tackle the problems he faced as a child. Now a senior street worker at the Institute for the Study and Practice of Non-Violence, Cartagena works with kids to keep them in school and out of gang life.

In the working class town of Lowell, Massachusetts, a man strides up the front stairs and through the metal detector of a solidly built, brick courthouse. Walking along the long corridor leading to the judge's quarters, First Justice Jay Blitzman passes a nervous looking group of alleged juvenile offenders waiting their turn in court. Everyday, Blitzman sits and tries a seemingly endless array of juvenile court cases, ranging from truancy violations to serious violent crimes. Like Gross and Cartagena, Blitzman has devoted his life to helping kids who face a wide array of difficulties. He was a public defender for more than 20 years and is the founder of the Youth Advocacy Project.

This school-to-prison pipeline shuttles children out of the classroom, where they are safe and monitored, and forces them onto the street, where they are more likely to commit crimes, or even worse, be killed. School dropouts are 3.5 times more likely than high school graduates to be incarcerated in their lifetime, and 68 percent of state prisoners are dropouts."[1] Blitzman said, "It is also important to emphasize that these problems are national in scope and directly related to the crisis in public education that has had profound ramifications regarding access to justice for children and their families. Fifty-four years after Brown v. Board of Education, the systems of public education for children of color and white children are still separate and unequal. Research has shown that in the majority of our major cities, approximately half of the children who enter ninth grade fail to graduate. A disproportionate percentage of these children are children of color and a disproportionate percentage of these children unfortunately later make their way into the juvenile and criminal justice systems. This process raises significant questions regarding issues of class and race in America. Tackling the problem is a public safety imperative."

So what is being done to fix the myriad of problems facing children in America's cities today? Teny Gross, David Cartagena and Jay Blitzman gathered together to discuss their different perspectives on the problem and to consider possible solutions:

Cartagena: I met a gentleman last Saturday. He is an alum from Brown [University]. He asked me, 'What can I do, as a Brown graduate, to help out with the kids in the school systems that you work in? Like, what can I do in these inner city public schools to make a difference?' And I said. 'You know to tell you the truth, you can show up. Let them see someone 19 to 20 years old not only in college but graduated from college. To them, that's a testament of success. They don't see that. I mean it might sound miniscule, but to kids it's like seeing a pro-athlete and it's not glorified enough. Sure the athletes are, the sneaker contracts are, the hip-hop rappers are, but the college education isn't. The college student isn't. You know, the pro-active college student that is in a social organization, that is in a fraternity, that cares about being, giving service back to the community. That's not glorified at all. You rarely ever hear of it unless you're on campus. You know what I mean? And I want to talk about education real quick.

But I'm going to say something first and equate it back to education. I was a couple of weeks on the job and, Teny remembers this 'cause he just happened to be with us this night, we were responding to a gang shooting with some YB kids and some mothers on Sackett Street on the south side of Providence. (YB is Young Bloods; the name of a gang.) And, as we get there, the police gang unit had already arrived. So there were regular officers, gang unit officers, and the sergeant of the gang unit, who runs that unit, sees me. It was my first few weeks on the job, and he says to Teny, 'What the fuck is he doing here?' So right away, what happened to me?

I'll tell you what happened to me, and then we'll equate this back to the educational system. What happened to me was, I went from feeling confident and confident about being able to help my community and making a difference and impacting the situation and being out there to do something constructive to all of a sudden feeling very incompetent and to feeling very ineffective and to feeling not socially accepted at all. [Since then the Sgt. has become a big fan of David's, added Gross.]

The reason why I bring that up when talking about education is because it reminded me of when I was a little kid. It reminded me of being socially deprived, economically disadvantaged, emotionally sheltered and going into a school and somebody telling you, 'perform this,' and you don't have any idea. So when you go into that public school system, there's nobody there to help you feel socially competent.

When you fail, it's your fault. Nobody takes that kid and says, 'What's the underlying issue? What's this kid's background? What's this kid's situation? Let's bring the kid's parents into school.' Around the time they get to doing that, is when they're already failing you.  It's when you've already jumped to the point of school refusal. Now, you're making excuses to not go to school. All of a sudden you're sick, and these physical symptoms are actually very legitimate because you can become physically sick because of those conditions. So, now you're making excuses not to come to school. So now, you're also labeled as a truant. But you're not. You're refusing to go school for legitimate reasons, but you're too young to voice your frustration and to voice your opinion about it. And now you're stuck.

And by the time you get to that court system, you have the wrong label. You have the wrong label. So how can we effect change in the educational school system? Empower them. No matter where they're from.

Blitzman: Here's an example, there's an alternative school in the city. It's a great school. I see kids there that I see in court. I can't go as much as I'd like because I'm not the lawyer anymore. I can't create a relationship with them because I am going to be adjudicating them. That's an ethical concern. But I see these kids as kids. I see them thriving, and I see a school that tries to get to them individually. And then I see the kids when they leave that school and go back to the big high school. All of a sudden, they're labeled again. And they can't shake that tag.

People don't get past the label. And we don't do enough diagnostics to understand what's going on. Some of the kids were described to me as the worst possible kids; they thrived in this school. What do they have? They've got people who are able to take the time. The school is small. They find a way to enfranchise, to empower, to understand, and these kids take off. They thrive.

I go to their Law Day. Every year, they have Law Day across the country, and this is the school I go to. And I don't talk about the theme of Law Day. I say, I'm here to answer any questions that you have. The question that I always hear every year is 'What's the best part of the job?' They also ask questions that really bring tears to my eyes. You know, there are some things that I can't answer. 'Is it easy for you to lock a kid up?' 'Is it easy for you to take a kid away?' We can send kids to prison for life in our juvenile court. We have done it a lot. These kids ask questions that go to the heart. These kids are asking about the most visceral things.

The question that always breaks my heart is 'Do you believe in second chances?'

And I've had the toughest kids say that with tears in their eyes. The kids who I went and saw with this program were being honored as students of the year. They were on the honor role. They're bright kids.

And tragically, I've seen these kids go from that environment back to the large high school, where they fall back.

Gross: It is very difficult to advocate the position he does in the legal system.

Blitzman: I've come to understand the pressures that under-resourced school systems are dealing with as well as the public safety implications of school drop out. Educators and juvenile justice professionals are in the business because we care about children. If you could do any one thing, I would advocate the implementation of a systemic tutoring system for any child who would avail themselves of that service. I believe that drawing on resources of college and university schools of education to create tutoring internships is a cost effective collaboration. We meet monthly in Lowell to explore such collaborations outside of the polarized context of court cases. The city's school superintendent and police superintendent attend regularly in an effort to maximize limited resources and address the complexities of the problem.

Interviewer: Dave and Teny, you guys are both here with these kids. What do you see? I imagine you do some form of mentoring or tutoring. Is that working? Is that hard to implement? Do you see it as a viable solution? Do you see alternatives?

Blitzman: Or does it even help?

Cartagena: The resources are not being invested. I mean sure, it costs a little more to lock somebody up, but it's a little easier too. Know what I mean? To try and get to the heart of

DISCOURSE

DO YOU BELIEVE IN SECOND CHANCES?
A ROUNDTABLE DISCUSSION INTERVIEW

NATHANIEL TEICHMAN

143

6 OF 10

the issues, to try to discover human nature, to care and not be desensitized to whatever it is they are going through, it takes a real person to get involved like that. And a lot of people just either don't have the time, don't care to have the time, or can't relate to this person on that level. Because this person is down here. This person is a throwaway kid.

That's how the system, I think, as a whole looks at a lot of these kids. The system looks at them like that. You know, I'd like to help the kid out, I'll throw him a dime here and there. But I don't want to invest in him. I'll give him a little bit of my time, but that's all I can do. And that's how it is.

But what you do is you nurture, you plant the seed. And now you grow somebody that can help your generation, and the next generation.

We live in a very materialistic culture. We live in a very violence-driven culture. So there is nobody there that has the human capacity and that love for humanity any more the way it used to be on the scale that it used to be. I mean I might sound like I'm from the daisy age or something right now. But it's true, it's what we need. It's what Martin Luther King Jr. talked about. "Love is the only force capable of transforming an enemy into a friend." I wholeheartedly believe that. I wholeheartedly believe that.

And kids aren't being taught that. Kids are being taught the complete opposite. Hate your fellow man because he don't care nothing about you. And if he sees you on the ground, he's gonna walk by and stomp on you as he's going by. So you take what you can from this life. So they grow up and know that it's every man for himself. And they gotta get what they can. And that's why you see the proliferation of violence and the way it's escalated to the extent where kids will chop your head off now. You know what I mean. Because it's what they are learning from the other generations, it's what they are learning from everyone else.

So it's up to us to bring it back to the basics, to bring it back to some normalcy, to extend ourselves to them. When I do presentations, people say, 'Wow you work with kids in gangs, you work with kids that are high at risk, you know, how is that?' And I say, what do you mean, I'm just a human being. I'm just doing something that an average member of the community should be doing. I'm just touching them with love. That's all I'm doing. It's what they want. It's what they don't get. It's what they yearn for. It's unavailable to them.

Blitzman: That's a powerful message. These kids don't get that.

A noted researcher, Kathy Spatz Widom writes about the cycle of violence. She compares children who are abused and neglected to baby crocodiles, who are abandoned at birth. She says the crocodile spends the rest of its life getting even. So you've got a lot of angry kids. It's not surprising. For me, some of the kids that I respond to the most positively, are some of the kids that people say have attitude problems. And you know, I'm in court and I see this kid and I see moxie and feistiness and I say, wow. I get excited. I get a little tingle that that kid has resilience. I'm thinking if I was in his situation I would be catatonic, gumming food in the corner. This kid might survive just in spite of well-intended do-gooders like me because this kid has something going on. Those are the kinds of kids that I think are the easiest to reach out to because there's something there and they want it, they want to be helped. It's important that we teach accountability but we have to be very intentional in how we deal with confrontational youth. We have to be more than merely reactive. Dr. Ross Greene, who wrote *The Explosive Child*, teaches that with confrontational children, a significant percentage of our delinquent population, we have to learn how to engage in a different manner, unless we want to re-create the very type of behavior we seek to avoid. Some of it is caring and some of it is training. But a lot of it, is thinking about doing things just a little bit differently.

Gross: C.S. Lewis said, 'Decent conduct doesn't pay to any particular person at any given moment. It pays to the whole human race as a whole.' So that really typifies the way I try to view life now. And it's the way that these kids really need to be touched. Because some kids, what they really need is they still need to be nurtured and to be brought up decently so that they won't go on to harm the next person, so that they don't go on to harm my mother, or your daughter, or your sister.

Interviewer: You can't really talk about what you can do with someone's family, it is the hand they are dealt, but what you are saying is that these schools are so important because they determine if the kids feel like abandoned crocodiles or empowered individuals. If you had the ear of any politician and their pocketbook wasn't struck by a financial crisis, what could be a possible game changer? What's failing in these schools, is it the size? Is it the competency of the teachers?

Blitzman: We are leaving every child behind because we haven't funded the initiative [No Child Left Behind].

Cartagena: I went to a school called Perry Middle School on Hartford Ave in Providence, so I was in that school from 1982-84. That school hasn't changed a bit. It's the same exact school, same building, which is like 100 years old. But what's changed is the ethnic makeup, the nationality of the school. It is now 83 percent Hispanic and probably 83 percent of teachers are Caucasians, so probably nobody understands the culture that these kids come from. You might have two ESL [English as a Second Language] teachers in the whole school. These kids, in my opinion, are getting the short end of the stick.

The school is doing what it's always done, they just haven't evolved with the community. The community is what's evolved. The community is more ethnically diverse, but the school staff is still 80 percent white you know. They don't understand that some of these kids are Guatemalan, Ecuadoran, Salvadoran, Venezuelan, Costa Rican. They don't understand the difference, they just lump them all together. When these kids are fighting, it's you know 'these two Spanish kids are fighting,' you know 'what are they

DISCOURSE

DO YOU BELIEVE IN SECOND CHANCES?
A ROUNDTABLE DISCUSSION INTERVIEW

NATHANIEL TEICHMAN

145

8 OF 10

fighting about?' You miss the heart of the problem, and it will be ten or fifteen years from now before the schools realize the problem. It will too late for the kids who have to live it today.

Blitzman: It's like in Lowell, you know they're all Asian kids, so there's no difference between Laotians, Vietnamese and Cambodians. Wrong. If you're a student of history, you'll see that you have 300 years of conflict.

Interviewer: How are you getting people in positions to understand, to see these conflicts and differences?

Cartagena: Well, I try to educate them myself, whenever I'm doing conflict resolutions or mediations within the schools. Whenever I'm sitting in and advocating for a child with his parent, and the child is facing a suspension or in-house focus, I sit there and I work hand in hand with the administration, with the principal. I keep them updated on every kid. I come in with the little street-level knowledge I have and I come out looking more important than they are. Maybe I should get that seven-figure salary they're making because a situation will arise and they won't have a clue about what it was about. I go, and I already have a prior relationship with the students, and I talk to them. I understand them. They trust me, and they know that I'm someone who cares about them. And there are not enough people like that in schools and that's the biggest problem. The kids will always gravitate and tell the truth to the person that they know cares, the person that really knows and has the interest in them. The person that's just there because they have a job and that's their salary -- the kids are gonna lie to them, manipulate them, connive them, get over on them.

Blitzman: I'm not Cambodian. We try to get street workers to come to court because they have a much better shot at making a connection then I'm ever gonna have. I like to get off the bench and sit down and talk to people. I remember doing this once in a case with a Cambodian family. So I was looking at somebody, and the guy is not looking at me. He's being evasive. And Keto Tan, the Khmer interpreter, said to me later, 'I know you were trying to do a nice thing, but you were being disrespectful to that family because he was trying to be nice by not looking at you. When you look someone in the eye, that's a very hostile, aggressive thing. That's very confrontational.'

Gross: It is not one thing that makes a kid successful. You need options.

I was a middle class kid growing up in Israel. When I no longer felt like building airplanes, I could try soccer. You need discipline, you need structure, you need love, and you need to be read to. We need to restore music. In Providence, Toshiba donated musical instruments to the school system. After a while Providence Schools called Toshiba and said thanks, but we've got to give them back to you. They are new I know, but we fired the music teachers, so we don't need the donated music instruments.

We get depressed if life has no beauty, if there is no purpose to it.

I'm sick and tired of those people not on the front line, not asking the important questions like: 'how many front-line youth workers does a city of a certain size and certain poverty levels need.' It's like a war orchestrated from the Pentagon; you aren't going to win unless you have soldiers on the ground. In Providence, we are trying to. It has been ten years, but its getting close, also because the economy is actually helping us. To actually make the juvenile jails smaller, kids go faster into halfway houses, that are going to have more programming and community. So those are positive, concrete juvenile reforms that are now being recommended. We have 'Kids Count' in Rhode Island, which has all the data and numbers on how kids are doing and how they are being fed and whether they have health insurance and food stamps. And together we are a really formidable advocacy coalition around the State House. I always said as a streetworker in Boston, 'If you are only working with kids, you are a failure. If you don't use what you hear from the kid to change the adults' mindset, you are really not advocating for the kids.' We need to change the rules.

Blitzman: One of the great things about the UTEC [United Teen Equality] program is the engagement that we have been talking about. When you go to a UTEC event, the whole thing is run by kids. They present, they introduce, and they lead. It's theirs. It's really about empowerment. They feel they own a piece of whatever it is. As opposed to us, the adults, telling them what is in their best interest. Which is huge. It's a different model of engaging kids. I mentioned Ross Greene. He's pioneered an approach called collaborative problem solving. He's consulted with the Maine juvenile correctional system to reduce the use of chemical and physical restraints by training staff how to interact with oppositional kids in a different way.

Ross Green will say, 'Kids who can, can; kids who can't, can't'. In other words, if I say to a kid if you don't do A, I'm going to lock you up. Well amazingly, a lot of kids don't do A. So the question is, is it because the kid is being a real jerk, or is it because there is a wiring problem or something that you have got to get behind? So Green talks about different ways to engage with kids, training staff to deal with kids so they don't have to use four point restraints, let alone chemical restraints. And the responses are generally very positive. Because again, it's a different kind of way of engaging kids. And it doesn't cost money. It's a philosophical approach.

Gross: Well, if the kid already feels he is already an empowered person, he can take criticism and he will do "A" work.

Blitzman: Here is another example. There are hundreds of thousands of kids in the Unified School district in LA County. They suspend over 7,000 kids a year. They've got this school-to-prison pipeline. They have huge gang problems. In 2007, they adopted a different type of school discipline policy, one that uses graduated sanctions. This was developed to try and combat zero tolerance and the School Board unanimously adopted it.

They did it out of desperation, because what they were doing wasn't working. It is too new to have measurable results. But you know if you can change a discipline policy in one of the largest school districts in the country, maybe there is reason to hope. Maybe this will work. There are programs that you can adapt and hopefully draw upon.

It's a question of using limited dollars wisely and investing in systemic approaches that better protect public safety and improving trajectories for kids and their families.

Cartagena: You can spend ten million a month to send guys in arms to another country, then you can probably spend two million a month to have guys defend this country. Preserve life in this country.  Like Teny said, $40,000.00 a year (per streetworker).  / END

NOTE FROM THE AUTHOR:

I FEEL INCREDIBLY LUCKY TO HAVE MET DAVID CARTAGENA. I ONLY KNEW HIM FOR A BRIEF PERIOD OF TIME. BUT IN THOSE FEW ENCOUNTERS HE TOUCHED ME WITH HIS INSIGHT. HIS STRENGTH AND HIS PASSION. SADLY. HE RECENTLY PASSED AWAY IN A CAR ACCIDENT IN PROVIDENCE. THE LOSS OF SUCH A MAN AS DAVID IS UNTHINKABLY TRAGIC. BOTH FOR THOSE HE LOVED AND INSPIRED AND FOR THOSE HE NEVER GOT A CHANCE TO INFLU-ENCE. THE TUFTS COMMUNITY WAS FORTUNATE ENOUGH TO HEAR DAVID SPEAK ABOUT YOUTH AND THE URBAN POOR DURING THE 2008 EPIIC GLOBAL POVERTY AND INEQUALITY SYMPOSIUM AND AGAIN IN 2009 WHEN HE ADDRESSED THE CHALLENGES OF URBAN CRIME AND VIOLENCE AT EPIIC'S "CITIES: FORGING AN URBAN FUTURE" SYMPOSIUM.

DAVID WAS TIRELESS IN HIS PURSUIT OF PEACE. HE SPREAD HIS INFECTIOUS ENTHUSI-ASM AND UNFLINCHING COMMITMENT TO NONVIOLENCE FROM PROVIDENCE. RHODE ISLAND TO PORTLAND. OREGON. REACHING ALL THE WAY TO ANTIGUA. GUATEMALA. CHARMING AND INTELLIGENT. DAVID WAS EQUALLY COMFORTABLE HELPING GANG MEMBERS TURN THEIR LIVES AROUND. A PATH HE HIMSELF FOLLOWED. OR CONVERSING WITH HEADS OF STATE AS HE DID DURING THE PROJECT ON JUSTICE IN TIMES OF TRANSITION'S "LEADERS OF THE PRESENT" CONFERENCE.

TODAY THERE IS A LITTLE LESS JOY. A LITTLE LESS LOVE. AND A LITTLE LESS COURAGE FOR US AS A COMMUNITY TO DRAW ON. DAVID WAS AN EXTRAORDINARY MAN WHO ROSE FROM DIFFICULT CIRCUMSTANCES TO MAKE A DIFFERENCE FOR EVERYONE AROUND HIM. HIS IMPACT AS A PEACEMAKER. AS A LEADER. AS A FATHER. AS A FRIEND AND AS A PERSON WILL NEVER BE FORGOTTEN AND TOGETHER WE MUST STRIVE TO KEEP HIS LEGACY ALIVE. DAVID OFTEN SPOKE ABOUT THE NEED TO REACH OUT AND TOUCH OTHERS WITH LOVE. DAVID LIVED THESE WORDS. ADVOCATING FOR KIDS THAT HAD NO ONE ELSE TO HELP AND ENCOURAGE THEM. NOW. WE AS A COMMUNITY MUST NOT ALLOW THIS RESPONSIBILITY TO GO UNFULFILLED.

DAVID WAS 38 YEARS OLD AND IS SURVIVED BY HIS PARENTS AND YOUNG DAUGHTER.

THE INSTITUTE FOR GLOBAL LEADERSHIP WILL BE WORKING IN CLOSE COLLABORATION WITH THE INSTITUTE FOR THE STUDY AND PRACTICE OF NONVIOLENCE IN SUPPORTING ACTIVITIES CREATED IN DAVID'S HONOR (WWW.NONVIOLENCEINSTITUTE.ORG).

– NATHANIEL TEICHMAN

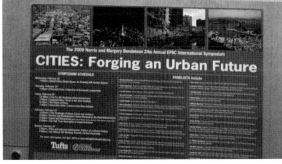

# NOTES F
# CHICAGO

Jesse Welch is an 18-year-old slam poet from Chicago and a first year student at Tufts. He was a finalist in last year's Louder Than A Bomb poetry slam and will be featured in an upcoming documentary. He has performed across the Midwest, at venues ranging from the Museum of Contemporary Art in Chicago to the Mexican Heritage Cultural Museum to Wendy's. His work has been published in *Say What! Magazine, Moe's Cafe,* and the Tufts Literary Magazine, *Outbreath*. He is currently a member of the Berklee College of Music Collegiate Slam Team.

# ROM A BOY

When our Bulls won the championship in 1991

We rioted

Years of frustration pouring from fingers in the form of fire

Torching cop cars and taxis

This was redemption

This was triumph

This was basketball

In 1992, after the repeat

We repeated

The morning after,

The taxis still resting on their hoods

Staring back

Still asleep like last night's bad decision

We slipped away to work

Doing our best to not wake their wreckage

In 1993, we rioted again

Just another championship

Just another riot

In '96 we rioted MJ's return

In '97 the greatest season in history

In '98 the end of an era

We burned victory into our city's memory

Came together in masochism

We were one in the flames

Burning used Camrys just as quickly

As Ferraris


This is how Chicago comes together

We are not a polite city

And we don't play well with each other


It is only in flames

That we find ourselves

And only in basketball that we find victory


On November 4th

As election results rolled in

And our native son cruised to victory

Every camera in the world focused on us

I watched Grant Park in fear

This was 1991 and 1968

This was Chicago

Coming together in victory

This was every cop in the city on duty

This was our two largest streets being shut down

This was a million Chicagoans lining the lake front

This was Southsider standing next to Northsider

This

Was our time to burn


The chants hit my bones like machine guns

He came to the stage a messiah

And turned fire into water

Bringing the city together in its tides

I watched as news cameras panned past

A kid in baggy jeans and a hoodie

Sobbin' on the shoulder of a white man

Still dressed in that day's suit


I didn't cry because Obama won

I cried because

Fire crews spent the night with their families

And cops cheered with the rest of us

We chanted

We screamed

We cried

And we went the fuck home

The next morning

Taxis did their job

Chicago threw a party

And the taxis stayed on their wheels

This wasn't change we could believe in

This was change


I come from a city of flames

Windy carrying of sparks into firestorms

This is not the first time I'm proud of my president

Or of my country

But it is the first time I've been proud of my city

We did not burn

Thank you Obama

You may not walk on water

But you are a damn-good fireman

# ART JUS PERMANE ENOUGH BEAUTIF

BEFORE THE WORLD REMEMBERS
HOW INSIGNIFICANT WE ARE

JESSE WELCH

DISCOURSE

ART JUST PERMANENT ENOUGH TO BE
BEAUTIFUL / BEFORE THE WORLD
REMEMBERS HOW INSIGNIFICANT WE ARE

JESSE WELCH

153

2 OF 4

We'd long since decided that the clack
Of the bead priming aerosol
Was the symphony Mozart was trying for
It was the sound of potential
And the hiss
Of paint escaping can
Was life's sweetest release

We were small time boys
Bombing run, acid-etch, marker job
We threw our mark upon the world
In the form of petty vandalism
Damaging it to difference

QWEST was different
When he first saw the wall
He'd found his destiny
Four stories up and forever wide
A ledge in front
Just wide enough for his high tops
And a drainage pipe leading up
That might hold his weight

"Every piece I've ever done is gone
They buff me before I've even split the scene
I'm trying to out paint monotony
But the world don't wanna change"

The whole crew swung by for support
He never looked down as he climbed
Just reached the ledge, unshouldered his bag
Took out a can
Shook up the world
And sprayed

DISCOURSE

ART JUST PERMANENT ENOUGH TO BE
BEAUTIFUL / BEFORE THE WORLD
REMEMBERS HOW INSIGNIFICANT WE ARE

JESSE WELCH

155

4 OF 4

Water blue lettering
Purple velvet highlights
Midnight blue lowlights
QWEST sprayed his soul onto city's canvas
Property-damaged it to beautiful

The sirens started before he had finished the outline
But his eyes never left his work
He filled in to the sound of cops blaring his end into
megaphones
Ignored the engine of approaching cherry picker
And made the operator wait
As he finished the shading

We all stared up at what he'd made
Some saw his name
I saw his life
The police saw property damage
QWEST
QWEST just smiled
Dropped his empty
Watched it fall from the heavens
Four stories to finished
He spread his arms in sacrifice
From art to infinity

Cops pulled them back to humanity
Wrapped his tools behind his back-
And QWEST smiled
Even as cuffs were slapped on
Tight enough to rub wrists raw
QWEST smiled
Looked every officer dead in their eyes
Asked them
Had they ever seen anything so beautiful

# DISCOURSE